The ABC of Sociology

UXBRIDGE TECHNICAL COLLEGE

KW-162-991

The ABC of Sociology

A series from *New Society*

Martin Slattery

MACMILLAN

© *New Society* 1979, 1980, 1981, 1982, 1983 except for
entries on pp. 4, 11, 13, 17, 22, 31, 34, 37, 42, 50, 73, 80, 109, 120

© Martin Slattery 1985

All rights reserved. No reproduction, copy or transmission
of this publication may be made without written permission.

No paragraph of this publication may be reproduced, copied
or transmitted save with written permission or in accordance
with the provisions of the Copyright Act 1956 (as amended),
or under the terms of any licence permitting limited copying
issued by the Copyright Licensing Agency, 33-4 Alfred Place,
London WC1E 7DP.

Any person who does any unauthorised act in relation to
this publication may be liable to criminal prosecution and
civil claims for damages.

First published in book form 1985
Reprinted 1987, 1989

Published by
MACMILLAN EDUCATION LTD
Houndmills, Basingstoke, Hampshire RG21 2XS
and London
Companies and representatives
throughout the world

Printed in Hong Kong

British Library Cataloguing in Publication Data
Slattery, Martin
ABC of sociology.
1. Sociology—Dictionaries
I. Title
301'.03'21   HM17
ISBN 0-333-39331-7

CONTENTS

ACKNOWLEDGEMENTS

The author would like to thank Michael Williams, Editor of *Society Today*, for his editorial help in compiling the original articles; also Paul Barker, Editor of *New Society*, for permission to reprint the articles in this form.

The author and publishers wish to thank the following copyright holders and Examining Boards for permission to reproduce copyright material and questions from past examination papers.

Thomas Nelson & Sons Ltd for an extract from *A New Introduction to Sociology* by M. O'Donnell.

Penguin Books Ltd for an extract from *Factory Time* by Dennis Johnson in *Work 1* edited by Ronald Fraser (Pelican Books, 1968).

Pitman Publishing Ltd for an extract from *Karl Marx: Selected Writings in Sociology and Social Philosophy* edited by T. B. Bottomore and M. Rubel.

The Associated Examining Board

Cambridge University Local Examinations Syndicate

East Midland Regional Examinations Board

Joint Matriculation Board

University of London School Examinations Board

University of Oxford Delegacy of Local Examinations

Welsh Joint Education Committee

The author also wishes to extend a warm 'thank you' to Cilla, Rachel and Ben for their support, encouragement and tolerance while their Dad was away 'scribbling'.

INTRODUCTION

This book is the complete series 'The ABC of Sociology' run by the magazine *New Society* in their schools supplement *Society Today* between October 1979 and May 1983. The aim of the series was to provide brief but clear definitions and explanations of the key terms and ideas in sociology today. The series was primarily aimed at 16-18 year-olds taking public examinations at O and A level, though *Society Today* was later added to the Open University booklist as a background resource for their Introductory Course in Sociology.

The aim of this book is essentially the same, but more comprehensive:

—The majority of the entries are those originally published but where necessary they have been up-dated and extended
—Fourteen extra definitions have been added to the original forty-four
—Each entry is cross-referenced with those other definitions that form part of a particular topic or debate
—The final section of the book provides examples of authentic examination questions at GCSE, O and A level set by all the Examination Boards that offer sociology as an exam subject.

This book is therefore more than just a dictionary of sociology. It is a comprehensive guide to the key terms, concepts and issues used at this level. It provides an overview of the important topics and useful material for exam preparation. The examination questions give a clear idea of the type and level of question asked at GCSE, O and A level and offer useful class/homework practice. The entries themselves are brief enough to be used for revision purposes. However, though the majority of entries are suitable for GCSE level students, several are obviously more appropriate for A level or advanced studies (e.g. Positivism, Phenomenology, Ethnomethodology). The level of language and types of concepts involved reflect this.

is for

ALIENATION

Factories may differ, but we are all suffering from the same industrial malaise. We are all second fiddles to machines. The loss of dignity and restriction of talent compatible with modern factory life cause a lack of quality in the factory worker. If the working man is to retain his sense of purpose some compensation must be made for the enforced boredom of the contemporary working condition.'
Source: *Work* by Ronald Frazer, Penguin Books

Hence demands for high wages, the high rates of absenteeism, and the number of strikes in many of today's mass-production factories. This sort of fatalism seems a strong feature of much of working-class life – the skilled, those in small family businesses and the middle classes seem to get more satisfaction from their work and their lives outside their jobs. They feel generally more involved.

Karl Marx was the first major sociologist to develop this concept and he used it as part of his critique of capitalism.

Alienation is a very complicated concept as it involves feelings rather than objects. At its simplest it describes the sense of frustration, pointlessness, isolation, lack of involvement, even hostility felt by many working in today's giant factories, especially under the discipline of assembly lines. Possibly the clearest way to illustrate it is in the words of a factory worker:

'People who speak grandiosely of the 'meaning' of work should spend a year or two in a factory. The modern worker neither gives anything to work nor expects anything (apart from his wages) from it . . . Time rather than content is the measure of factory life. Time is what the factory worker sells: not labour, not skill but time, dreary time . . . sold to the man in the bowler hat. The end product provides no consolation to anyone who works in a factory. It is the factory, not what is made, that makes factory workers what they are. There is something about factory life that is inconsistent with man's progress through time: something retrograde.

'In what does this alienation of labour consist? First, that the work is external to the worker, that it is not a part of his nature, that consequently he does not fulfil himself in this work but denies himself, has a feeling of misery, not of well-being, does not develop freely a physical and mental energy, but is physically exhausted and mentally debased. The worker therefore feels himself at home only during his leisure, whereas at work he feels homeless. His work is not voluntary but imposed, forced labour. It is not the satisfaction of a need but only a means for satisfying other needs. Its alien character is clearly shown by the fact that as soon as there is no physical or other compulsion it is avoided like the plague. Finally, the alienated character of work for the worker appears in the fact that it is not his work but for someone else, that in work he does not belong to himself but to another person.'

Source: *Selected Writing in Sociology and Social Philosophy* by Karl Marx, ed. T.B. Bottomore and M. Rubel (Watts). Reproduced in *Sociological Theory, A Book of Readings*, ed. L.A. Coser and B.M. Rosenberg (Collier-Macmillan)

Thus in Marx's view, work in a CLASS society is not a source of self-expression, creativity and pride but a commodity judged solely in terms of its saleability. The worker feels isolated not only from his own work but from his fellow-workers, the customers and his employer. Relations in a capitalist society are those of competition ('dog eat dog') even amongst the workers, rather than cooperation. Profit, rather than human need is the prime consideration as the bourgeoisie seeks to exploit both the workers and the customers. Marx believed that in a communist society where the means of production were communally-owned, exploitation and class rule would end, and work, far from being a source of alienation, would again become a means of self-expression, a liberation of the human spirit and imagination.

In the 1950s and 1960s American sociologists, noting the growth of absenteeism and strikes in American factories, analysed alienation as a psychological rather than sociological concept (or a criticism of the capitalist system). Robert Blanner, for example (*Alienation and Freedom*, 1964), broke the concept of alienation down into four basic elements − POWERLESSNESS, MEANINGLESSNESS, ISOLATION and SELF-ESTRANGEMENT − and argued that certain types of technology were particularly alienating. Thus he saw the modern assembly line as extremely alienating, work in process plants such as chemical plants less so and craft work, as in say printing, as deeply satisfying because the worker is his own boss and controls the whole task. Such workers work as a team and take considerable pride in their achievements. Blanner saw the introduction of automation, however, as a source of liberation, freeing workers from boring, repetitive and mindless tasks. It allows them to see over the whole work process and to feel in control of the machines rather than being controlled by them as before. Other writers, especially neo-Marxists, are less optimistic. They see automation merely as an advanced form of exploitation which does nothing to alter the relations of production. The control and ownership of modern work is still in the hands of the bourgeoisie and in many ways the workers have even less power. Their particular skills − and often even their jobs − have been replaced by machines. Such writers similarly see other experiments to reduce alienation, such as job-rotation, team production and even worker-participation, as having only a temporary and cosmetic effect. They remove the worst aspects of assembly-line work but still leave real control in the hands of the owners, not the workers, and relationships between the two are still those of exploiter and exploited. Even where the workers actually run the factories as in Yugoslavia and 'employ' managers symptoms of alienation are evident.

Thus in its truest sense the concept of alienation refers to the whole social structure. It can be applied equally well to the sense of frustration, powerlessness and isolation felt by many people in all areas of modern life − in dealing with modern bureaucracy or government, in living in huge estates of high-rise blocks, in being unemployed. To many 15 or 16 year-olds even school is an alienating place. Instead of feeling a sense of purpose and place, they come to feel lost, frustrated, even failures. Like adult workers, most resign themselves to such boredom, some hit back with misbehaviour, even vandalism, in an attempt to express themselves or to re-establish some sense of control over their lives and achieve some status.

Though revolutionaries in China, Cuba and elsewhere have sought to create truly ▶

liberating societies, few have so far succeeded. With the growth in all forms of organisation, particularly government and bureaucracy, alienation in modern life seems likely to increase.

See also DIVISION OF LABOUR.

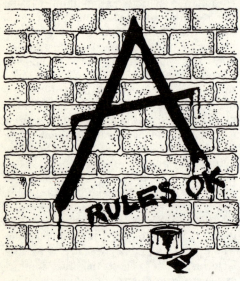

is for

ANOMIE

Whilst sociologists refer to the generally accepted forms of behaviour in a society as its NORMS (see page 68), anomie is most simply defined as NORMLESSLESS – as a breakdown or absence of commonly-agreed values and standards. Anomie may thus refer to:

—a widespread disagreement, questioning or rejection of society's central value system

—a situation where there is a collapse of social consensus (as in, say, Northern Ireland or the Lebanon)

—or one where the social controls that enforce and maintain social conformity weaken or collapse.

The concept of anomie derives mainly from the work of the French sociologist Emile Durkheim and more recently from the American writer Robert K. Merton. Durkheim described social solidarity in pre-industrial societies as 'MECHANICAL' based on a commonly-agreed set of goals and values, clearly defined and strictly enforced in such small-scale communities. He described social solidarity in industrial societies, though, as 'ORGANIC', as more intricate and tenuous because, though in such large-scale societies there exists a general consensus over goals and values, it is far less clearly defined and less easily enforced. The emphasis on individual rights, the growth of sub-cultures and the variety of views as to what is right and socially acceptable all lead to a questioning of society's norms and values. Whilst Durkheim recognised that such developments could be 'functional' and constructive, helping society adapt and offering directions for change, he also feared that industrialisation could lead to the collapse of society through both the speed of change involved and the ever-increasing division of labour. Such factors create a whole spectrum of individual 'worlds' and encourage individualism and self-interest. As social controls weaken with the change of industrial-urban society and as individual desires and appetites are stimulated beyond measure by the prosperity of industrial progress, it becomes more difficult to foster any sense of collective responsibility or commitment to society at large. To Durkheim such a situation is not only dangerous for society at large but for the individual too, because it leaves him morally blind, uncontrolled and directionless. Normlessness in society is therefore a source of 'sickness'; when goals outrun means, when individuals' expectations are unrestrained, then crime and suicide become more likely. The type of suicide where people kill themselves because the guidelines or norms of society have broken down, Durkheim called ANOMIC suicide. It is most likely to occur during periods of economic boom or depression like the 1929 Wall Street Crash, when society is in a state of flux and old standards are being rejected for new.

Robert Merton modified this concept to analyse crime and deviance in advanced industrial societies. He saw the lawlessness, deviance and unrest evident in modern America as being the result of a lack of fit, or a conflict between, the common goals of American society — the 'American Dream' of becoming a millionaire, President or simply materially successful — and the opportunities available to achieve this. Whilst all Americans are socialised into striving for the top, quite obviously only a few can actually make it. The vast majority must accept some form of failure and adapt to it. Such adaptations may involve some form of deviance, for example, failing to achieve the 'American Dream' by legitimate means, some turn to crime as the avenue to wealth and success. Others adapt to the American Dream by either withdrawing from the race for success and retreating into an alternative lifestyle (hippies, drug-addicts) or by rejecting the competitive and materialistic values of capitalist America altogether. Some radical groups such as the Black Panthers and Minutemen have gone so far as to plot armed revolution to overthrow the American state. Thus for Merton, anomie — and so deviance — are the result of a mismatch between society's goals and its opportunity structures. In Durkheim's analysis greater emphasis is put on the breakdown in the moral order of society. Despite extensive criticism, both interpretations have had a powerful influence on both sociology and on policy-makers, as evidenced by the variety of programmes to 're-educate' juvenile delinquents and 'problem' families and to try to increase opportunity for groups at the bottom of society — for example the Headstart Programme in American in the late 1960s. Some have analysed football hooliganism, mugging and other forms of mindless delinquency as examples of anomie.

See also NORM(S), DEVIANCE, ALIENATION, COMMUNITY, DIVISION OF LABOUR.

hoped. They are often criticised for being too conservative, and for creating endless printed forms, many of which are unintelligible to the general public. They are accused of being insensitive in the way they treat people, especially the homeless, the aged and unemployed, and most especially of being too powerful.

Faceless bureaucrats seem to be making all the decisions in society and taking none of the responsibility. This increases people's sense of powerlessness and of

is for

BUREAUCRACY

Bureaucracy refers in its narrowest sense to the officials and civil servants who run today's modern government. In its broadest sense it covers all forms of administration, from the local comprehensive school to hospitals, trade unions and even the local football team — they all need people to run them. As modern government has expanded its responsibilities, it has needed to employ more and more civil servants to run such major services as health, housing and, of course, taxation. This growth in size seems to be happening to all major organisations.

Max Weber, the nineteenth-century sociologist, believed the most efficient way to run an organisation was to choose officials solely according to their ability, to give them specific tasks or duties to be carried out only according to a specific set of rules and regulations: and to organise them in a sort of chain of command or hierarchy, with the officials above controlling those below. Thus Weber hoped to ensure organisations ran smoothly without favouritism or abuse of power — though he was also fully aware of the potential dangers of bureaucracy.

Unfortunately bureaucrats are not always as efficient and dispassionate as Weber

alienation. Mrs Thatcher's electoral promise to cut down on the civil service was a popular one — though its officials and unions are resisting it. Within sociology, Weber's Ideal Model of Bureaucracy has proved an endless source of controversy and debate. This debate has centred on two main issues: the efficiency of bureaucracy; bureaucracy and democracy.

(a) *The efficiency of the bureaucratic model*

(i) Robert Merton (*Bureaucratic Structure and Personality*, 1957) identified a number of dysfunctions of bureaucracy — its inflexibility, the ritualistic adherence to rules and regulations even if the rule was obviously misguided; bureaucrats' conservatism, lack of imagination and inability to innovate. The division into specialised departments further leads to department loyalties and conflicts that threaten the smooth running of the whole organisation.

(ii) Peter Blau (*The Dynamics of Bureaucracy*, 1963) showed how informal methods used by employees are often more efficient than the formal ones of going by the rule book – and they enable employees to avoid the scrutiny of their supervisor! Michel Grozier has shown how this can lead to increasing rigidity as supervisors apply more rules to ensure that they control their workforce – and the workers find new methods to avoid such scrutiny.

(iii) Studies like Alvin Gouldner's of a gypsum mine (*Patterns of Industrial Bureaucracy*, 1954) and Burns and Stalker (*The Management of Innovation*, 1966) of the electronics industry showed that whilst bureaucracy is a suitable form of organisation in situations where production is routine and predictable, it is totally unsuitable for those requiring initiative, flexibility and innovation.

(b) *Bureaucracy as a form of social power or control*

Are bureaucratic organisations inevitably undemocratic? Is bureaucracy a threat to democracy?

(i) Weber was aware of the danger of bureaucracy, to democratic government. Their control of information, their traditions of secrecy and anonymity make civil servants unaccountable and give them considerable influence over their political masters, the politicians. However, Weber put his faith in the ability of Parliament to control such power.

(ii) After studying the apparently most democratic of organisations (trade unions and socialist parties) Robert Michels was far less optimistic. He proposed the IRON LAW OF OLIGARCHY (*Political Parties*, 1911) that though organisation was essential to democracy as the only way individuals in large-scale societies can effectively make themselves heard, inevitably in time, the leaders of such organisations come to dominate and control its decisions more in the interests of preserving their own powers and privileges than in pro-moting those of their members. Thus he argued, 'Who says organisation says oligarchy'.

(iii) Many studies since have agreed with Michels and some modern writers like Brian Sedgemore, Tony Benn and the Crowther-Hunt Report have even argued that the British Civil Service is a form of ruling class.

(iv) Despite the many attempts to increase democracy in all walks of life – worker-participation, the Bullock Report, pupil power and Freedom of Information Acts – progress has been limited. Even socialist countries and experiments like the Israeli Kibbutzim have not established true democracy, in the sense that everyone has a say, let alone an equal voice.

Sociologists have also developed different perspectives or views on how modern organisations actually function.

Functionalists such as Talcott Parsons tend to see organisation as a key feature in the functioning of the modern social system. They tend to portray them as 'things' with almost a life, even a personality, of their own, e.g. we often talk of say British Rail almost as a living organism (sociologists call this REIFICATION). Internal conflicts tend to be ignored in such studies and efficiency highlighted as in say the Scientific Management approach. Such an analysis of the functioning of organisations tended to dominate sociology and such disciplines as Business Studies up until the 1960s.

Recently – during the 1970s – Marxist writers have applied their conflict perspective to this area. They see the bureaucratic structure of modern organisations not as a means to efficiency but to control by management of the workers/employees. Such control is ultimately class control – the middle classes over the workers – and part of the means by which the bourgeoisie control all aspects of modern life. The modern citizen lives in an organisational society. 'We are born in organisations, ▶

BUREAUCRACY (continued)

educated by organisations and most of us spend much of our lives working for organisations ... Most of us will die in an organisation and when the time comes for burial, the largest organisation of all, the State, must grant official permission.' (Amitai Etzioni, *Modern Organisations*, 1964)

The question is who controls such organisations and in whose interests? Interactionists tend to analyse the effects of life and work in organisations on the individual. Erving Goffman's study of TOTAL institutions like asylums (1968) is a classic example of the effects of life in a closed environment.

C is for CAPITALISM

When a country industrialises – develops a system of production based on industry, factories, machines and towns with all the resultant changes in such social institutions as the family, religion and the government – a complex system of production, exchange and distribution is involved. This can either be centrally planned and organised by the government as in Soviet Russia or it can be left to the efforts of private individuals held together by the invisible hand of the market forces of supply and demand. This latter system is called CAPITALISM. Individuals with sufficient capital start and run their own businesses (factories, farms, mines, banks, services), employ workers for as low a wage as possible and seek to sell their products for as much PROFIT as possible. Profit is used not only to increase personal wealth but to expand businesses and/or invest in new enterprises. Workers sell their labour freely on the LABOUR MARKET for as high a wage or salary as they, their skills and their union can command. The essence of this economic system is competition between firms in order to sell their goods to as many people as possible, to make greater profits and to expand, possibly to such an extent as to take over a particular market and so establish a MONOPOLY. Under such *laissez-faire* capitalism, the role of the government is merely to ensure law and order and to give business a free hand.

Those who support this capitalist economic system believe that competition and the PROFIT MOTIVE stimulate natural desires for self-improvement, ensure that businesses are highly efficient, give the individual the opportunity and freedom to fully develop his or her talents, and enable a society to enjoy ever-increasing wealth and a continually rising standard of living; without in their view, all the dangers and hindrances of central government control and bureaucracy.

Many, however, have criticised this system as being so unjust as to be immoral, allowing the few to become very wealthy at the expense of the many, and basing human relations on the CASH NEXUS and exploitation instead of cooperation. Probably the most thorough and devastating criticism of nineteenth-century capitalism was that of Karl Marx (see MARXISM, p. 61). Inspired by his ideas many developing countries have chosen the Soviet model of industrialisation as both quicker and fairer − though critics see it merely as STATE CAPITALISM.

Countries such as Britain, America and most of Western Europe industrialised over the past 150 to 200 years on the *laissez-faire* model. Some, though − like Germany and Japan − learning from the experience of Great Britain, used the state to 'encourage' industrialisation by subsidising and protecting key industrial sectors, providing financial aid and even by setting up state-owned companies. Modern or WELFARE CAPITALISM, as Britain has today, is characterised by:

1 A great expansion of the role of government not only to regulate the worst abuses of private enterprise but to provide a WELFARE STATE to ensure that no one suffers absolute poverty. Similarly the government has taken over or NATIONALISED certain key sectors of the economy such as coal, gas and the railways to ensure that they are operated efficiently and in the common interest. Some writers see such central control as so extensive as to constitute a CORPORATE STATE (state control of the economy).

2 Today few major companies are owned and run by one person or family. The modern firm is usually owned by SHAREHOLDERS and run by a Board of Directors. Though individuals often own shares, the majority today are controlled by such large institutions as banks, insurance companies and pension funds and/or by huge conglo-merates and MULTINATIONAL corporations controlling a wide range of firms and industries. Such control and ownership has reached the point where many markets or industries today are dominated by a single firm (a MONOPOLY) or a few firms collaborating together (OLIGOPOLY).

3 The growth of a large and ever-growing MIDDLE CLASS, i.e. people occupying key positions in the structure and administration of capitalist societies − bankers, executives, solicitors, teachers. Generally they enjoy a high standard of living and a certain social status. They are therefore usually opposed to radical change in the existing social system.

Historians and social scientists have argued extensively over the origins and necessary pre-conditions for capitalism.

(a) From his theory of history as a series of economic stages or epochs Karl Marx saw capitalism as the MODE OF PRODUCTION that followed feudalism and preceded socialism. He saw it as progressive because it created the means to economic abundance; he saw it as unjust because it involved the exploitation of one class by another, an exploitation that would finally lead to social revolution.

(b) Max Weber was less radical and utopian. He argued that cultural and political factors were as important as economic ones in industrialisation. He saw the driving force, the 'spirit' of capitalism in Western Europe, as the PROTESTANT ETHIC, the religious values of hard work, thrift, deferred gratification and a belief that 'the Rich shall inherit the earth', that wealth is a sign of God's favour. This individualism and willingness to take risks he saw as the spark that led to the industrial 'take-off' in Britain and Northern Europe.

(c) Modern analyses of capitalism, especially by Marxist writers, however, ▶

CAPITALISM (continued)

see it as an INTERNATIONAL system with two hundred or so major multinationals controlling the world market and determining how and if a Third World country industrialises. Huge conglomerates such as Ford and Dunlop are beyond the control of any one country and their market strategies involve moving production, even whole factories, from one country to another if they feel it is necessary to break a strike or get cheaper labour. Hence the closing of many factories in areas like Merseyside and their re-opening in such Third World countries as Korea. Some writers describe this control of the world economy by the multinationals and First World countries as a modern form of IMPERIALISM. Imperialism was also a key feature of the industrialisation of many West European countries. Britain in the eighteenth and nineteenth centuries, for example, had a huge empire which provided her factories with cheap raw materials and ready-made markets for the goods she produced.

Britain today is a classic example of the debate over the advantages and disadvantages of capitalism as an economic and social system. The present Conservative government's policies of MONETARISM and PRIVATISATION are part of a strategy to limit government involvement in the economy and to increase the influence of private enterprise and market forces (even in such areas as health and education) as the main means to reviving prosperity. The cost is mass unemployment and greater inequalities in the distribution of wealth. The Labour Party stood at the 1983 election on a programme of increased government planning and expenditure to revive the economy and employment – and suffered its worst electoral defeat ever.

See also DIVISION OF LABOUR, MARXISM.

is for
CASTE

A system of social stratification that originated in India. It is based primarily on religious purity but often also reflects divisions of occupation, wealth, power and status. The word caste derives from the latin CASTUS meaning clean, pure or pious. The key features of the caste system are:

—A highly formal and ritualistic system of religious ranking
—A system of ASCRIBED rather than ACHIEVED status by which you are born into a particular caste and cannot move up or down during your lifetime. It is thus a CLOSED or hereditary system of stratification with no formal avenues of social mobility.

The main castes are kept rigidly apart and represent distinctly different lifestyles. Cross-caste marriages, and even physical contact between castes are strictly forbidden. Caste membership thus determines not only occupation and social status but marriage partner, income residence, even

appearance and dress. Different castes must be able to recognise each other and so maintain social distance.

The classic example of the caste system is the Hindu system of traditional India. This system existed for some 3000 years and continues today despite attempts by the British colonial government and governments since to eliminate its restrictions and practices. The five main castes or VARNA are:

1 The BRAHMINS or priests and religious men
2 The KSHATRIYA or warriors and landlords
3 The VAISYA or merchants and farmers
4 The SUDRAS or peasants and manual workers
5 The HARYANS or Untouchables, social outcasts

The essence of this system is ritual purity with the Brahmins as the most pure, wise and holy and the Untouchables as the most unclean. The Untouchables are therefore given the dirtiest jobs to do and are segregated from the other castes. If even the shadow of an Untouchable is cast across the path or food of a member of a higher caste, extensive cleansing rituals are necessary. Whilst the Brahmins and *Kshatriya* are the wealthiest and most powerful groups, the Untouchables are the poorest and weakest. Each caste is subdivided into thousands of JATIS or subcastes each with its own restrictions and rituals. For the mass of the people living in villages, it is these social categories that are the most important determinant of their lifestyle and social status.

Officially no social mobility is possible save through the Hindu belief in KHARMA or reincarnation. If a person lives a pure life, strictly obeying his caste's code or DHARMA, then he may be reborn into a higher caste. Equally those who fail to keep their *Dharma* are liable to rebirth into a lower caste. The 'purest of the pure' who are elevated through successive reincar- ▶

CASTE (continued)

nations, may eventually be released completely from this cycle of deaths and rebirths. In practice some very limited social mobility is allowed through:

—*Hypergamy* where on marriage a woman may be allowed to move up into her husband's caste
—*Sanskritisation*, a process by which a whole group may gain ceremonial elevation by religiously imitating the customs and rituals of a superior *jati*, even to the point of looking down on those of previously equal *jatis*.

For sociologists, especially those from western societies where the rights of the individual, legal and political equality and achieved social mobility are so important, such a rigid system of social stratification is perceived as both fascinating and unjust. Fascinating in the sense that such a system has dominated so large a country for so long with little apparent change – even the Untouchables seem to accept their poverty, exploitation and degradation in the hope of a better life in the future – and unjust in the sense that to westerners, used to a considerable amount of freedom and equality, the caste system looks like a means of gross class exploitation whereby religion is used as an 'opiate' of the people, lulling the masses into submission and legitimising the extreme wealth, power and privilege of the few at the top of Indian society.

Some writers have attempted to apply the concept of CASTE to other forms of social stratification where some form of purity (racial, religious, sexual or social) and rigid segregation is evident. The segregation of blacks in the southern states of America and under the apartheid system of South Africa is one example; the position of women, even in modern societies, argues Helen Mayer Hacker, is another. Both women and blacks, she argues, are 'highly visible' and so easily excluded from positions of power, treated as inferior, discriminated against and kept in their place at the bottom of society.

See discussions on class, ethnicity and gender for alternative analyses of social stratification.

See also CLASS, ETHNICITY, GENDER, FEUDALISM, STATUS.

occupation as the simplest, most practical and most effective means of encompassing the wide variety of economic and social elements that go to make up a person's or group's class — their education, status, income and power.

is for # CLASS

Social stratification in one form or another is the central theme, the bread and butter of sociology because it is a key factor not only in the structure of society but in the behaviour, lifestyles and lifechances of its members. Social class is the main form of social stratification found in industrial societies. It is based primarily on ECONOMIC factors, in particular on OCCUPATION.

Most descriptive classifications of class or socio-economic status have relied on

'The backbone of class structure, and indeed the entire reward system of Modern Western society, is the occupational structure,' argues Frank Parkin. The most widely used of such classifications is that used by the Registrar General, which divides the British population into five main classes with the division between manual and non-manual occupations (social classes IIIN – IIIM) as the borderline between MIDDLE CLASS and WORKING CLASS.

Sociologists often use the more refined seven-point classification devised by Hall and Jones in 1950. Such classifications have, however, been subject to severe criticism:

1   Such scales reflect a middle-class

	Social class	Examples of occupations
	MIDDLE CLASS	
I	*Professional occupations*	*Doctor, dentist*
II	*Intermediate occupation (including most managerial and senior administrative occupations)*	*Executive, teacher*
IIIN	*Skilled occupations (non-manual)*	*Clerk, policeman*
	WORKING CLASS	
IIIM	*Skilled occupations (manual)*	*Printer, electrician*
IV	*Partly skilled occupations*	*Machine operators, farm worker*
V	*Unskilled occupations*	*Labourer, cleaners*
Other	*Residual groups including, for example, armed forces, students, and those whose occupation was inadequately described*	

▶

assumption that non-manual work is superior to manual.

2   They are based primarily on the occupation of the head of the household. They therefore assume that households have heads, usually assumed to be men, and so tend to ignore or undervalue working women. The mass unemployment of the 1980s raises further problems of the classification of non-workers.

3   They ignore the most powerful in society, the tiny minority who own land, property and capital but who do not work in the normal sense of the word.

4   With the growing similarity in terms of income, lifestyle and status of the lower middle class and the upper working class, the non-manual/manual division makes less and less sense.

5   Such classifications are based on OBJECTIVE indices of class, factors that can be relatively easily identified and measured, such as education and income. They do not take into account SUBJECTIVE factors, peoples' consciousness of belonging to a particular class. This raises major problems for the sociologist when people see themselves as being of a different class to that which they would objectively be allocated. For example, the worker who sees himself as middle-class and acts accordingly by, for instance, voting Conservative. This occasional lack of fit between the 'fact and consciousness' of class has raised major problems for such theoretical analyses as the EMBOURGEOISEMENT THESIS (see p. 30).

Despite such criticisms and problems, despite the present shift in the occupational structure away from manual towards white-collar occupations, few sociologists doubt the continued importance of social class on people's behaviour and lifestyles. In virtually every field the middle classes do better than the working classes (in health, education, housing, etc.).

The three main theories or perspectives on this form of social stratification are:

A   The **functionalist** view that social stratification is not only inevitable but functional. An unequal distribution of rewards and privileges as found in the class system of advanced industrial societies is the means by which society attracts its most talented members to take on the most important roles. Because the system is seen as MERITOCRATIC (see p. 64), the less able and unskilled in society accept both their lowly positions and the privileges of those at the top. They recognise that it is the interests of society as a whole that the most able make the key decisions. Thus, according to writers like Talcott Parsons, through a system of stratification, society is able to function efficiently and the underlying structure of order, cooperation and value consensus is preserved.

This model of social order and role allocation has been severely criticised as both inaccurate and conservative. Melvin Tumin has severely questioned the assumption that the class structure of advanced industrial societies like America is either meritocratic or efficiently organised. The functionalist model, he argues, ignores the influence of power, race, gender and home background in determining who gets the top jobs. Moreover it contains no mechanism for identifying the positions in society that are the most functionally necessary and so deserving of the highest pay and status. Should the chairman of ICI really receive twice or three times the pay of the Prime Minister? Are dustmen and nurses as unimportant to the efficient functioning of modern society as their low pay would seem to indicate?

B   The **Marxist** analysis of class is

radically different. Far from seeing co-operation, harmony and order as the underlying features of advanced capitalist societies this perspective highlights its inherent conflicts and contradictions. Far from seeing occupation as the basis of class, Marxists argue that the only real division in capitalist societies is that between those who own the MEANS of PRODUCTION and those who do not. Their model thus identifies only two main classes: the bourgeoisie and the proletariat – though such minor groups as the petty bourgeoisie and the lumpenproletariat are occasionally referred to. Social change occurs primarily through class exploitation and conflict which leads ultimately to social revolution and the structural economic change from a capitalist to a socialist and eventually communist society. A classless society will only be achieved when the means of production are communally owned. (For a fuller outline, see MARXISM, p. 61).

The working class will become conscious of its OBJECTIVE class position once it has moved from being a 'class in itself' to a 'class for itself' through the organisational unity and common exploitation of factory work. The failure to date of the classes in late capitalism to clearly polarise into two major groups, the growth rather than decline of middle class(es) and the lack of collective consciousness of the working class(es) has raised major problems for Marxist theoreticians. Explanations for such failures of prediction include:
(i) the concept of FALSE CONSCIOUSNESS (the continued inability of workers to recognise their class exploitation and objective position) and
(ii) HEGEMONY (the power of the bourgeoisie to control people's ideas and thinking to the point where capitalism is not only accepted as inevitable but natural and just – the power of the media, education and legal systems). Nevertheless belief in the ultimate polarisation of classes and of a class conflict is reflected in such recent theories as the PROLETARIANISATION THESIS (p. 85).

C   Max **Weber's** analysis of class is both a rejection of and a refinement of much of Marx's analysis. He too saw class in economic terms and saw the key division as that between those owning property and those who do not. However, for him the key determinant of a person's class position, of their lifechances – particularly the propertyless – was their MARKET situation. Those with greater skills, education and the like will be in greater demand in a capitalist society and so able to command higher incomes, higher standards of living and greater control over their lives. Those who share a similar MARKET position and enjoy similar lifestyles constitute a class and he outlined a hierarchy of classes as follows:

1   The propertied upper class
2   The propertyless intelligentsia and white-collar workers
3   The petty bourgeoisie of small businessmen and shopkeepers
4   The working class

His analysis differs from Marx's in certain crucial respects:
(a) He rejected the idea of economic determinism, that economic factors alone constitute the only basis of class, social inequality and power or historical change.
His analysis of the Protestant ethic and its influence on industrialisation was an attempt to show how cultural and religious factors were also important in historical development. He rejected the idea of the inevitability of socialism and saw communism as utopian.
(b) He accepted the idea of class conflict and exploitation but not to the same extent or in the same way as Marx. He rejected the idea of capitalist society eventually polarising into two major classes, identifying rather a hierarchy of classes and an expansion rather than ▶

CLASS (continued)

contraction of the middle classes. Similarly he identified a variety of other sources of class conflict other than simply economic exploitation, some of which fragmented as much as united classes such as race, status and party.

(c) He rejected the idea that class is the only basis of POWER, arguing that STATUS AND PARTY are equally important. Groups form not only because of similar economic positions but also of similar status situations and the distribution of such social honour often cuts across class lines. Moreover in his view, status often forms a stronger basis for group consciousness than class.

By PARTIES he meant groups aiming to influence social decision-making and so included both political parties and pressure groups, organisations that often represent a variety of classes and status groups.

Such a refined and complex analysis of class, however, is difficult to use as the basis of a research project or sociological theory because it offers such a variety of factors upon which to identify a person's social position and because the picture it paints of class in modern societies is so fluid and changeable. It has been further criticised as failing to give sufficient weight to the small but powerful minority of property-owners at the top of advanced capitalist societies. Nevertheless it has become an important basis for non-Marxist analyses of class.

Both Marx and Weber saw contemporary society as capitalist (see p. 8) and both saw the key features of its social stratification as the private ownership of the means of production and a market for labour. Whilst Marx emphasised the first, Weber emphasised the second; whilst both paid attention to class consciousness, Weber put greater emphasis on subjective factors. Both represent theories, rather than just descriptions, of social class.

The alternative to a stratified or class society has not yet been achieved. Even in Kibbutzim (see p. 54) and 'socialist societies', inequalities based on bureaucratic power, gender or ethnicity continue to arise.

See also CASTE, EMBOURGEOISEMENT, ETHNICITY/RACE, GENDER, MIDDLE CLASS, SOCIAL MOBILITY, STATUS, WORKING CLASS.

A sense of place has, similarly, been behind most sociological analyses of 'community'. From Emile Durkheim's concept of Mechanical and Organic Solidarity and Ferdinand Tonnies' of

C is for COMMUNITY

GEMEINSCHAFT-GESELLSCHAFT, a whole tradition of Community Studies developed within sociology. Though these two founding fathers never said that location was crucial to particular types of social relationship, most sociologists within the tradition of Community Studies did and they produced a mass of extremely detailed studies of every aspect of life in communities as far afield as 'Middletown' (America), County Clare (Ireland) and Yucatan (Mexico) — their kin-networks, powerstructures, rituals and even gossip networks. Underlying this tradition was the theory that

The term 'community' is one of the most meaningful and yet one of the most elusive words in the sociological dictionary. In fact one sociologist, George Hillery, found that even as far back as 1955 there were over 90 different definitions. In everyday use, 'community' is a word that conjures up the sense of belonging, intimacy and human companionship that comes from being a member of a group or society where there is:

1   a common identity and
2   a common set of values.

1   all communities could be placed in a line or continuum stretching from extremely rural to extremely urban communities
2   such communities represented totally different ways of life.

Such a communion of ideas and lifestyles has usually been associated with a particular geographical location. Thus we talk of community centres or community schools and take immense interest in the lives of people who live in communities such as Coronation Street and Emmerdale Farm. We use the term 'community politics' to refer to groups of local people who spring up to defend their way of life against 'faceless' bureaucrats, plans for slum clearance or a motorway. The town planners of the 1960s even tried to recreate a sense of community by the way they designed the New Towns and tower blocks of that period.

Rural life was depicted as one in which there was a strong sense of community based on PRIMARY relationships that were face-to-face, intimate and based on a strong sense of social order in which the family and the church were key social controls. Urban life was best depicted by the Chicago sociologist Louis Width in his essay 'Urbanism as a way of life'. He saw modern cities as so large, varied and densely populated that relationships were inevitably more SECONDARY — more impersonal, superficial, transitory and segmental than those in small communities. ▶

COMMUNITY (continued)

Whilst it is all too easy to feel alone, friendless and alienated amidst the hustle and bustle, the teeming crowds of New York or London, you could never feel lost in a small country village. ROLE RELATIONSHIPS are similarly very different. Whilst in rural societies they are very 'diffuse' and varied, in urban areas they are highly 'specific', linked to one specific task or contract. Compare for example the highly personal relationships of the 'village bobby' with the people of his community to the more fleeting, impersonal and specific contacts of the urban policeman in his panda car with the people on his 'patch'. Similarly compare the relationships of the village shopkeeper with his customers and the supermarket cashier with hers. Likewise the SOCIAL CONTROLS seem much tighter in rural communities — there is less to steal, everyone 'keeps an eye on everyone else' and strangers are quickly spotted. Amid the thronging masses and anonymity of the 'Naked City' social controls seem weak and crime easy.

Underlying such comparisons was the assumption that life in rural communities was better, more intimate and fulfilling than that in the city and that the urbanisation of the nineteenth and twentieth centuries had destroyed our traditional sense of community. It implied that *where* you lived DETERMINED *how* you lived and that therefore the 'Good Life' was most likely to be found in rural communities.

However, by the late 1960s this thesis was under severe attack as:

1 Studies like Young and Wilmott's of Bethnal Green in East London (1962) revealed the existence of 'urban communities' in the middle of large cities.
2 R.E. Pahl's study of 'commuter villages' in Hertfordshire (*Urbs in Rure*, 1965) revealed communities split by bitter conflicts between locals and the newcomers who had 'invaded' their villages in search of the Good Life. Simply moving to a village didn't make you a villager.
3 Researchers like Raymond Williams (*The Country and the City*, 1973) destroyed the myth of life in pre-industrial England being a Golden Age of Community. Life in medieval villages was anything but idyllic. It was harsh and oppressive as the great landlords exploited the peasantry as a means to perpetuating their own wealth and privilege. The appearance of community was a false one based on the 'mutuality of the oppressed'. As Williams argued, the differences between urban and rural ways of life are not a result of location but of the different impact of capitalism which obviously has a greater effect on life in the city than that in the isolated village.

Studies like these destroyed the concept of an urban-rural continuum and led most sociologists to conclude that the term 'community' was impossible to define, was too overladen with romantic overtones to be a useful and objective sociological concept — though some attempt to revive it was made by Professor Margaret Stacey's proposal that it be used for the analysis of 'local social systems', kin networks, power structures and the like. However, whatever academics may say the quest for community is not dead amongst the general public, as evidenced by the flight of people from the modern city to the peace and quiet, the human companionship of country villages, coastal resorts and even isolated communes.

See also URBANISATION, ANOMIE.

is for
CULTURE

would be considerably different.

A key characteristic of culture therefore is the fact that it is SHARED, and a key mechanism for such sharing, for transmitting the ideas and values of a particular society is LANGUAGE – written and oral. A society's culture guides – if not controls – its members' ways of thinking and acting; often unconsciously as we take our society as normal and our culture for granted. A culture is also a particular society's way of solving common problems, of making sense of the world. Cannibalism may seem barbaric to western eyes, but to many people it is their way of honouring the dead.

Culture can thus be seen as the 'skin' or fabric of society, binding together not only its individual members but its major institutions by providing a common set of goals and values.

This very consensual and holistic view of culture derives from functionalist theories of society (see FUNCTIONALISM, p. 40) and such a perspective dominated sociological ideas in this field in the 1950s and early 1960s. Recently this idea of core culture, extended and elaborated by a variety of SUB-CULTURES (see p. 112), has been severely challenged.

Conflict theorists such as Weberians, and especially Marxists, see modern mass society not as a united community with a single agreed set of values but as a wide variety of often conflicting cultures held together by some form of imposed order or consensus through such ideological controls as the mass media, education and religion. Such perspectives see even high culture (art, music, literature) and mass culture (TV, pop music) as ideological, as a form of class control.

Interactionists, by contrast, see the ▶

To most people the word 'culture' is used to describe the best of the arts – ballet, theatre, opera, classical music and the like. But sociologists and anthropologists use it in a special way to refer to the total way of life of a particular society – its members' customs, traditions and rituals, their attitudes and beliefs, their dress and language, their behaviour and relationships, the way they view themselves.

The particular culture of a society has developed throughout its history and is transmitted from one generation to the next. Thus we can talk of American, Eskimo and Chinese culture. People brought up in Britain have learnt a particular way of life, a particular set of values and attitudes, a pattern of behaviour that distinguishes them from Africans, Europeans, Japanese or South Americans.

Such cultures are learnt, not inherited. All children are born with certain characteristics inherited from their parents and a tremendous capacity for learning. How they develop greatly depends on the particular culture and/or sub-culture they are born into. Had you been adopted at birth by the Queen or by an Indian family your behaviour, attitudes, dress and so on

CULTURE (continued)

culture of a particular society – or the sub-culture of a particular group – as an expression of human creativity rather than as a form of social control. In their view people in their everyday interactions create and re-create the culture(s) of their particular group or society rather than having their way of life and values imposed upon them from outside.

Most societies, especially large complex ones, are thus made up of many groups, many 'ways of life' many layers of culture – conflicting, contrasting and overlapping. The great variety and richness of human cultures provide a constant stimulus for social scientists.

See also NORMS, SUB-CULTURES.

PB

is for
DEMOCRACY

Democracy is a much-used and much-abused political term. Countries as diverse as the United States and communist East Germany (the German Democratic Republic) claim to be democratic. The word itself comes from the Greek *demos*, meaning people, and *kratos*, meaning power. In the words of the American President Abraham Lincoln, democracy should be government of the people, by the people, for the people. The city-state of Athens in ancient Greece is often cited as an ideal example of direct democracy where all the citizens met together in the market place, discussed the issues of the day and reached decisions – truly self-government among equals.

However, in today's mass societies of millions of people it is obviously impossible to operate direct democracy, so indirect forms have been adopted. In the liberal democracies of the west we elect representatives, such as MPs and congressmen to make our decisions for us – a form of government by consent with the power of the government kept in check by opposition parties, a free press, and especially the need to stand for re-election. Decisions are usually made by majority vote, and the rights of individuals and minorities are protected by the rule of law.

The key features of liberal democracy can be listed as:

1 Free, fair and periodic elections on the basis of universal suffrage

2 The right of any adult (with certain exclusions) to stand for public office and such offices to be open to all

3 A minimum of two parties competing

for power to ensure that the electorate has a real choice of alternative government

4 A separation of powers to ensure no one body or person controls all three major branches of government – the Executive, Legislature and Judiciary

5 Decisions made on the basis of majority vote but protection for the rights of the minorities

6 The recognition and protection of certain key freedoms and civil liberties, in particular: *freedom of the press* to criticise government without fear of repression; *freedom of public association* to demonstrate peacefully against government decision, to form pressure groups and opposition parties; *freedom of the individual* against arbitrary arrest.

To date such political freedoms and forms of communication have only really flourished in societies where there are no serious divisions of wealth, religion or race. These are generally countries with relatively high levels of education, tolerance and stability like America, western Europe and Australia. Such freedoms rarely exist in the poor nations of the Third World.

Socialist and communist writers, however, do not believe that real democracy can ever develop while wealth and property are privately owned and unequally distributed. In their view, the rich and better educated inevitably have a greater say in government than the mass of the people and use such power to promote their own interests and profits. According to these writers, the alternative is to abolish CAPITALISM (see p. 8) and to establish SOCIAL DEMOCRACY under which the state in the name of the People takes over the means of production (factories banks, land, etc.) and operates them in the interests of all, not just the profits of the few. Once economic and social equality have been established, then and only then can all people participate fully and equally in political decision-making. Most communist countries are still at the stage of 'dictatorship of the proletariat'. Socialist parties in such western societies as Britain aim to achieve power by the ballot box rather than by revolution; and developing countries, faced by extremes of wealth and exploitation, often find a form of social democracy more suited to their historical and cultural background of dictatorship and poverty. However, the price of such promises of economic prosperity and equality is that in such communist countries 'political' freedoms are so far relatively limited. Few of the conditions listed above exist and the governments of such countries are often self-perpetuating dictatorships.

Ultimately the structure of democracy and the way it operates in a particular country depends on its interpretation of the key values of justice and freedom. The communist view of democracy emphasises fraternity and equality; liberal democracy highlights freedom and competition. Many writers, however, doubt whether true democracy will ever exist – even in Athens they had slaves and refused women the right to vote. Arguments over democracy are of increasing importance to all spheres of life – from Tony Benn's criticisms of democracy in the British Labour Party to the Bullock Committee's report on work-participation in industry. Democracy is but one form of decision-making – one that has to be guided and nurtured if it is not to slip into oligarchy and dictatorship. It may be a slower method of getting results, but at least people feel they have some say in decisions affecting them, some control over their lives.

See also ELITES, POWER.

DEMOGRAPHY

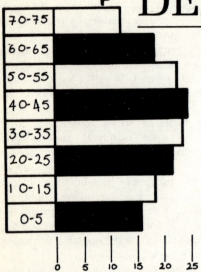

Age	
70-75	
60-65	
50-55	
40-45	
30-35	
20-25	
10-15	
0-5	

0   5   10   15   20   25

Demography has been defined as 'the scientific study of human populations with respect to their size, their structure and their development' (*The United Nations Multilingual Demographic Dictionary*, 1958). The term 'demography' was first used by the Frenchman A. Guillard in his textbook *Eléments de Statistique Humaine*, 1855. Its central concern is the establishment of reliable statistics on such factors as birth and death rates, marriages and divorces, migration, life expectancy and so on. Though censuses date back thousands of years, only recently has their definition and collection been sufficiently reliable to be considered scientifically accurate. The following are some of the key definitions in demography:

BIRTH RATE (Crude) The number of people born per 1000 population per year

DEATH RATE (Crude) The number of people who die per 1000 population per year

INFANT MORTALITY RATE The number of babies per 1000 live births who die under the age of one, per year

LIFE EXPECTANCY The further number of years that a man or woman might expect on average to live when he or she has reached a certain age, assuming present death rates stay at the same in the future.

MIGRATION The movement of people WITHIN a particular country (internal migration) or BETWEEN countries (external migration)

Immigration: people COMING INTO a country and settling there

Emigration: people LEAVING a country to settle elsewhere

DEPENDENT POPULATION The number of people unable to work who depend on others (especially on the family and on the state) for financial support. The main dependent groups in today's society are schoolchildren, pensioners, the unemployed, non-working wives and those on state benefits

WORKING POPULATION Officially defined as 'those gainfully employed of all ages and occupations including persons working on their own account as well as employees.' It includes all those insured and registered for work. It thus includes members of the Armed Forces and those registered as unemployed but not housewives or those who retire early.

The size of a particular country's population, the likelihood, strength and direction of future changes, all involve an intricate balance between such factors as birth and death rates, life expectancy and migration. Today, for example, the Third World is experiencing a 'population explosion' as a result largely of a dramatic fall in the death rate with the birth rate remaining high and life expectancy increasing. By identifying the key factors behind population change governments can try, if necessary, to alter such imbalances. China for example is at present trying to restrict couples to having only one child each. A detailed analysis of the structure of a country's population in terms of its distribution by age, sex, region and so on enables a government to plan ahead in terms of, say, the number of schools or roads. At present more countries, especially the advanced ones, are having to tackle the problem of an ageing population, of how to find money for the growing number of old age pensioners from a declining workforce.

Government interest in population statistics until the twentieth century was mainly limited to taxation and the collection of armies. With the growth of the welfare state and the need to plan a modern economy, governments today digest a regular diet of facts and figures on education, housing, health, etc., fed to them by ten-yearly censuses and annual surveys. Scientific interest in demography also has a long history, particularly since Thomas Malthus published his famous *Essay on Population* in 1798, in which he said that the world was about to starve to death because whilst population tends to increase geometrically, food supplies grow only arithmetically.

Although that was an overpessimistic analysis of his own time, the present population explosion has led to a revival of such ideas (neo-Malthusianism) about the imbalance of world resources and population. Demography as an academic discipline tends to concentrate on facts and figures and the lack of theories about how populations grow and change has led to the recent development of the sociology of fertility and other analyses of the social factors involved in for example the greater life expectancy of women than men in most societies (but not all). Similarly the recent work of the Cambridge Centre for the Study of Population and History has brought the study of demographic data of the past to the forefront of sociological analysis and theory, as for example in the work of Peter Laslett showing that the nuclear family was as much a feature of pre-industrial societies as it is of modern ones.

 is for

DEVIANCE

Usually deviance is defined as behaviour that is considered abnormal or unacceptable by a particular group or society, behaviour that deviates from its NORMS or LAWS. Deviant acts range from quite innocent ones, like nail-biting or stuttering, to serious crimes like murder and theft. Thus from such a view it can be said that all crime is deviant, but not all deviance is criminal.

The Sociology of Deviancy grew up in the 1950s and 1960s as a reaction to the traditional assumptions in criminology that:

1 deviancy and crime were the same thing

DEVIANCE (continued)

2 criminality was explainable solely in terms of criminals, that deviancy was an individual characteristic, even that certain types of people were criminal-types due to personality defects or the backgrounds they came from

3 official statistics on crime were the real facts, a true picture of crime and criminals in our society

4 the norms and values of advanced societies were generally agreed upon and accepted by everyone.

Deviancy theorists reached a much broader view and definition.

Using mainly an interactionist perspective they sought:

(a) To distinguish between deviant acts, such as foul language, and those people labelled as deviants, such as skinheads or lunatics

(b) To examine the relative nature of this concept. In their view no act is inherently deviant, e.g. to kill someone may be considered good (as in war) or bad (murder). What may be considered deviant in one situation may be normal in another, e.g. wearing a bikini in church. What may be deviant in one society, may be normal in another, e.g. drinking alcohol in Britain as compared with Saudi Arabia. What may be deviant in another age may be normal today. Imagine, for instance, wearing mini-skirts in Victorian times.

(c) To question the assumption that modern mass societies are governed by a common value system by pointing to the variety of sub-cultures — and so of conflicting norms and values — that exist.

(d) To analyse the processes by which people are labelled deviant. In Howard Becker's view 'deviance is behaviour other people so label'. But obviously certain groups have more power to apply such labels than others. For example, the mass media greatly influence such notions as 'the bizarre face of punk' and 'dole scroungers'.

It takes a doctor or psychiatrist to authoritatively label someone as sick or mentally ill, a policemen or judge to declare someone a criminal. Once they are so labelled, and especially if they are 'put away', criminals, lunatics and patients are more likely to act the part. Some sociologists, especially Marxists, go further and believe that through its control of the economy, government and media, the 'ruling class' makes laws and creates norms and stereotypes to protect its own interest and property. Thus, they say, it is inevitably the lower propertyless classes who are mainly labelled deviant and criminal.

(e) To highlight not only the inaccuracies in official crime statistics but the social processes by which they are created, they challenged the official picture of crime as a minority activity and of the typical criminal as young, male, working-class and living in a city. Rather, through self-report studies and victim surveys they showed:

(i) that crime is in fact a widespread activity

(ii) that those who enter the official statistics and get caught only represent the 'tip of the iceberg' (about 15% of all crime) and are an unrepresentative tip at that. They only represent the 'unlucky and the inefficient', those that get caught and those that fit the policeman's stereotype of a typical criminal. The old, female and middle-class are generally ignored or treated more leniently.

(iii) that an increase in the crime rate may not necessarily reflect an increase in the activity of criminals but of the police, the public, the media or the politicians. By reporting more crimes the public 'increase' the crime rate; as do politicians by making more laws. When there is an increase in the police force, more of the 'Dark Figure of Crime' is discovered, as more crimes previously unknown come to light.

Such a broad analysis of deviance took in not only crime but any form of abnormal behaviour from football hooliganism to stuttering. It highlighted the way the social control agencies (police, courts, politicians) often 'create' crime and deviancy by the way they REACT to certain situations or groups especially via LABELLING (see p. 57). Leslie Wilkins proposed in 1964 the idea of 'deviancy amplification' that exaggerated attention by the media or the police of a particular group or area, turned them from relative insignificance into 'Folk Devils'. A public outcry, a 'MORAL PANIC' (Stan Cohen) develops over such stereotyped images (e.g. of football hooligans) and a sort of 'spiral' develops as the group concerned lives up to its public image and the attention it is accorded, so 'proving' the image correct and encouraging greater public denunciation and police attention.

Deviancy theory (like labelling) is criticised, however, because:

1 It implies that merely labelling someone deviant or criminal makes them so

2 It fails to explain who has the power to label, why some groups escape labelling. Marxists, for example, see such power and the control of the police, courts and legal system as crucial elements in the ability of the bourgeoisie to defend property and their own interests and keep the potentially rebellious working class under control. The middle classes run the police, courts, etc. and the concentration of such social controls on the workers is 'justified' by official statistics that apparently show crime to be a working-class activity and that 'white-collar' crime is negligible. According to Marxist analyses, though, the really big criminals are the businessmen and politicians at the top, those who use bribery and corruption to increase their wealth and privilege but who are too powerful to be prosecuted.

3 Its definitions are often so woolly that some sociologists like Michael Phillipson have argued that the term 'deviancy' is so imprecise that it should be eliminated from the sociological 'dictionary' altogether.

4 It may explain minor deviances and crimes such as drug-taking and sexual offences but it is of limited value in explaining serious ones like murder because murderers are only 'labelled', and only face a 'reaction', after the crime. Further, the concentration by deviancy studies on such 'underdogs' as prostitutes and petty criminals leads to them ignoring the top dogs, the professional criminals, in it by choice.

Nevertheless this approach dramatically challenged traditional views and offered new and stimulating insights not only into the behaviour of criminals but those trying to control them. It also led to the application of such concepts to non-criminal areas, to a consideration of how groups like the physically and mentally disabled are labelled, how the reaction of 'normal' people isolates and affects such people and so in a sense makes them feel deviant or odd. Feminists have argued that women who do not fit the typical feminine stereotype – who go out to work, do not get married – also find themselves labelled, stigmatised and set aside as deviant by men and by such processes women are kept under control and in their place. In a school it is the headmaster backed up by his staff, who decides what is normal, what is deviant and what the rules are to be. Teachers label pupils as bright, average or failures not only by the way they treat them, but under a streamed system, according to the class they put them in. Some sociologists see this as a self-fulfilling prophecy, with upper-stream pupils becoming successes and lower-stream pupils failures.

See also LABELLING, INTERACTIONISM, PHENOMENOLOGY.

is for

DIVISION OF LABOUR

Division of labour is a very important term in sociology – so important that Durkheim used it as a title to one of his key works. In the narrowest sense it is an economic concept referring to the organisation of work, the division of a particular task into a number of separate specialised jobs as a means to increasing productivity and efficiency. In its broadest sense it refers to the whole structure of relations – between the classes, the sexes – in industrial societies.

1 *The economic division of labour* stems from the nineteenth-century economist Adam Smith's idea of specialisation and he gave the example of a pin factory to show how by dividing up into stages even the simple task of making pins, productivity rose enormously. Other Free Trade writers of this period argued that by each country specialising in the areas they were best at and trading freely with other nations, all would benefit from the greater output, quality and lower cost. Division of labour along such lines has been a key factor in industrial countries through the factory system being able to produce abundance where before there was scarcity. However, mass production tasks are now so subdivided that it is now relatively easy to replace men by machines (e.g. robots in modern car factories).

Mechanical production is obviously faster, more reliable (and less likely to strike), than an ordinary workforce. Automation means that machines can be coordinated and controlled by computers, with raw materials fed in one end and the finished production rolling out the other. Under full automation, only a few workers are required to programme and supervise the machinery.

The advantages of this industrial division of labour are enormous in terms of immensely raising our standard of living by mass-producing vast ranges of goods cheaply. Its disadvantages primarily affect factory workers faced with boring repetitive tasks requiring little skill and providing little job satisfaction. They come to feel ALIENATED (see p. 2) and their dissatisfaction is expressed in high rates of absenteeism, sickness and/or strikes and industrial sabotage.

The extensive division of labour, the structure of modern factories, and the use of assembly lines since the days of Henry Ford's Model T in the early twentieth century stem largely from the SCIENTIFIC MANAGEMENT ideas of F.W. Taylor. His analysis of even the minutest task into its most basic components is popularly called TIME AND MOTION study and was an attempt to increase the efficiency of every worker. Marxist writers like Harry Braverman (*Labor and Monopoly Capital*, 1974), however, see such a technique as a means to DESKILLING workers, to reducing worker involvement, skill and control to the point where it is easy to control the workforce and to replace it by machines and robots. Union resistance to such trends has produced some limited experiments at reintegrating the production process and worker control (e.g. team work in Volvo factories) but the overall trend is to automation replacing workers.

2 *The social division of labour*

(a) Emile Durkheim saw the division of labour as the key feature distinguishing primitive societies from modern ones. In pre-industrial societies a low division of labour and face-to-face relationships produced MECHANICAL SOLIDARITY, whilst the extensive division of labour and more impersonal and distant relationships of industrial societies produced a complex system of interdependence: ORGANIC SOLIDARITY, with tasks and roles based more on 'contractual' relationships.

(b) Karl Marx saw the economic division of labour as primarily that between those who owned the means of production and those who were propertyless. Such a division formed the basis of his social classes and underlay class conflict and exploitation. He further saw the division of labour in industrial factories and places of work as part of this class exploitation and control and also the source of the sense of ALIENATION felt by many workers (see p. 2). Modern Marxists like Harry Braverman and Graeme Salaman argue that the division of labour in modern organisations such as factories or bureaucracies is not a means to increased efficiency but in fact a means to increase management control of the workforce because when worker involvement is reduced and worker isolation is increased the worker is easier to control and replace.

(c) Feminist writers have concentrated their attention on the sexual division of labour arguing that it is not natural or biological but essentially cultural and represents a structure of power (patriarchy) by which men rule women in both the family and the workplace (see Gender, p. 42).

A high degree of specialisation seems to be a key characteristic of all aspects of industrial society, affecting not only the workplace but government and even the home. As Durkheim predicted, people's 'worlds' are increasingly narrow and disconnected, producing in extreme cases ANOMIE or normlessness (see p. 4).

See also ALIENATION, ANOMIE.

occurred through a 'circulation of elites' – as one elite grew over-confident and decadent it was subverted and replaced by another. He saw the mass of the population as apathetic. Morca divided society into two classes, a small superior ruling class and the mass of people, the ruled. Unlike Pareto he saw the type of elite in power as varying from society to society and also came to recognise the potential of modern democracy for the people to control their leaders, though he never approved of such popular government.

(ii) Robert Michel's analysis of such apparently democratic organisations as

is for ELITE(S)

In the broadest sense, an elite is a group in society considered to be superior because of the power and privilege of its members. Elites can be found in all spheres of life – religion, education, the military and so on. But sociologists are particularly interested in 'political' elites, their composition and ability to influence or control the rest of society: the rule of the few over the many.

The Sociology of Elites is an age-old area of political debate and analysis:

(a) Classical Elite Theory stems from the writings of Italian sociologists Vilfredo Pareto (1848-1923), Gaetano Mosca (1858-1941) and Robert Michels (1876-1936) all of whom saw elitism as inevitable, even desirable in modern societies, given the limitations of the mass of the population.

(i) Pareto and Mosca analysed political elites in terms of their personal qualities. Pareto identified two main types of governing elites, the LIONS – who were powerful and decisive and who ruled by force as in military dictatorships; and the FOXES – cunning and able to manipulate European democracies. Political change, he argued,

trade unions and socialist parties (in Germany) led him to the IRON LAW of OLIGARCHY that 'whilst democracy is inconceivable without organisation', 'who says organisation says oligarchy'. Thus he saw modern democracy as inevitable – not because of the rule of the few.

(iii) Karl Marx also saw elitism as inevitable but not because of the qualities of certain individuals but because one class has always controlled the means of production, and so had power over the rest. In capitalist society this economic elite is the bourgeoisie (see Marxism, p. 61). The theories of Pareto, Mosca and Michel attempted to disprove Marx's analysis and especially his prediction that such elitism would disappear in communist societies when there was no private ownership of the means of production.

(b) Modern versions of this debate generally come under the title of PLURALIST-ELITIST controversy as to the distribution of power in advanced capitalist democracies. Both sides accept the existence of elites in all walks of life (business, unions, etc.) but disagree about whether such elites compete or cooperate; whether they are 'open' or 'closed'.

ELITIST writers believed that modern societies are controlled by an all-powerful group, a sort of ruling class or establishment, 'which dictates policy for the rest of the nation' (N. Crockett in *The Power Elite in America*, 1970). Thus, ordinary people feel unable really to influence the government. According to C. Wright Mills, the American power elite comprises three distinct but allied elites: the military, the owners and the managers of the large corporations.

Another view of the British power structure by A. Aaronovitch, sees financiers as being in control of the state. They make decisions which affect the welfare of millions of people without being accountable to the electorate.

In contrast, PLURALIST writers see the power structure as much more fragmented and fluid. Instead of one unified elite controlling political decision-making, they believe political decisions are made through a process of competition and conflict among many groups with varied interests − with the government acting as a sort of referee or broker. Their analysis of decision-making (for example Robert Dahl's study of New Haven in America, and Christopher Hewitt's of the British government's policies between 1944 and 1964) shows no one group dominating government decisions.

Elitists reply by referring to NON-DECISION-MAKING, the ability of very powerful groups to prevent issues that threaten their power and privilege ever reaching Parliament or Congress. They are so powerful that they control the political agenda and exclude discussion on, say, poverty, race or the distribution of wealth. One recent attempt to resolve this debate is Thomas R. Dye's study *Who's Running America?* (1979) in which he sought to identify the actual individuals and families who would form the ruling class in America today and how they coordinated their control. Though he concluded that the elitist case was partially proven, it was not completely substantiated.

Studies of other societies are generally equally inconclusive. Communist societies are certainly elitist in their political structures but are such elites governing solely in their own interests? David Lane thinks not (*Politics and Society in the USSR*, 1976). However even Kibbutzim, set up to establish pure democracy, seem to reveal oligarchical tendencies with men and the more educated dominating top positions (Eva Rosenfeld, *Social Stratification in a Classless Society*, 1974).

Elite analysis also necessitates study of the 'masses' and though elitist writers in the classical tradition had little faith in the 'people', modern elitist writing tends to argue for greater popular involvement.

See also DEMOCRACY, POWER.

bridge University Press, 1968) — an investigation of highly-paid workers at Vauxhall, Laporte Chemicals and Skefco. If true, the embourgeoisement thesis had to prove that such workers:

1 were economically equal to the middle classes
2 held attitudes and values identical to those of the middle classes
3 were accepted as social equals by the middle classes.

Goldthorpe and Lockwood emphasised that manual and non-manual workers were not alike in economic terms. Though their incomes were often similar, manual workers received no 'perks' or annual increases, lacked job security and any real

is for

EMBOURGEOISE-MENT

Though used by Karl Marx to refer to factory owners and other capitalists, the term 'bourgeois' is usually used to describe the middle classes — doctors, civil servants, lawyers, businessmen and so on. The 'embourgeoisement thesis' is, therefore, based on the belief that ultimately we will all become middle-class.

Research has concentrated on the 'affluent' working class, e.g. car-workers and miners, who enjoy incomes comparable to those of many middle-class occupations, and so seem likely to adopt a middle-class lifestyle — buying their own homes, investing their money and developing a nuclear-type family structure. This thesis gained popularity in the early 1960s through such writers as Tony Crosland, David Butler and Richard Rose as an explanation of Labour's persistent failure to win an election in the 1950s.

The most important study in this area is that by John Goldthorpe and David Lockwood (*The Affluent Worker*, Cam-

chance of promotion. Goldthorpe and Lockwood also failed to find any evidence, not only of affluent workers being accepted as equals by the middle classes, but also, more important, of their wanting to be.

For them high wages were considered more important than job satisfaction, and they looked for real meaning in their lives at home and in their leisure. Goldthorpe and Lockwood concluded that rather than an embourgeoisement process taking place, such workers represented a new PRIVATISED working class with an INSTRUMENTAL attitude to work and a 'privatised' one to life outside, including such so-called middle-class behaviour patterns as joint-conjugal roles and a considerable interest in their children's education and job prospects. However, though they lacked the unity and class-consciousness of such traditional workers as miners, they too saw society in terms of US and THEM rather than as a ladder anyone could climb. Hence their support for the two main organisations promoting the collective power of the working class – the trade unions and the Labour Party.

Though it was written – and criticised – in the 'affluent' sixties, several writers still believe that there is a future for the embourgeoisement thesis, not simply because the growth of the white-collar sector produces 'a shift of the occupational structure from the shape of the pyramid to that of an electric light bulb' (A.H. Halsey), but because the micro-chip seems likely to eliminate most forms of manual work. So, by definition, we will all become non-manual – or unemployed.

In a re-analysis of this thesis, Ken Roberts (*The Fragmentary Class Structure*, 1977) identified a bourgeois section of the working class – manual workers owning their own houses, living on middle-class estates, opposed to trade unions and voting Conservative. 'The bourgeois worker is a living animal,' Roberts says, but represents a minor not a major group within the working class.

Moreover the General Elections of 1979 and 1983 in which a Tory Government was elected with the support of many workers, especially skilled workers living in the South East of England (see PSEPHOLOGY, p. 87), added further fuel to this debate.

See also **MIDDLE CLASS, PROLETARIAT, WORKING CLASS.**

is for

ETHNICITY AND RACE

The term ETHNIC derives from the Greek work *ethnos*, a people, and was originally used to refer to a nation, particularly a pagan one. However, in common usage it has become synonymous with race. Socio-logists and anthropologists, whilst recognising that these two meanings overlap, argue that they should be considered separately. Thus in the social sciences, whilst 'races' are distinguished ▶

by their biological features (e.g. Mongolian, Negroid, Indo-European), ethnic groups have a specific cultural identity. Ethnicity is thus a very broad term that can cover whole nations or peoples such as the British or Jews as well as smaller groups with a common language, customs and beliefs such as Rastafarians and Australian pygmies.

In the American census, for example, people are officially classified by both race and ethnicity with such major racial categories as black and white sub-divided by ethnicity into those of hispanic origin and those not. In so diverse a society as the USA such intricate classifications are crucial to a clear understanding of race relations since racial groups often include a variety of ethnic sub-cultures; for example, Irish-Americans are ethnically distinct from Italian-Americans but both are racially distinct from Black Americans. Moreover whilst relations between such ethnic groups are fairly equal, those between blacks and whites constitute a form of social stratification, of inferiority and superiority. A similar situation can be identified in Britain today with blacks as a body suffering racial discrimination but relations between such ethnic groups as Sikhs and West Indians being relatively equal. The classic example of racial stratification today is the apartheid system of South Africa where segregation is openly legitimised and legally enforced.

Thus, though ethnicity rarely implies any sense of inferiority, such cultural distinctions can develop into a form of PREJUDICE — a pre-judgement or predisposition to think, feel or act favourably or unfavourably towards a particular group or its members without adequate knowledge or experience. Such views or feelings are often irrational but occasionally have some basis such as a fear of loss of jobs or overpopulation. Prejudice can therefore lead to

social conflict and discrimination, especially once the particular features of an ethnic group's lifestyle become STEREOTYPED (see p. 111), the subject of jokes (e.g. the stupidity of the Irish, the meanness of Jews) and/or given such derogatory labels as 'micks' or 'dagos'. This is especially likely during periods of social crisis or economic depression when the dominant racial and ethnic groups are looking for scapegoats.

The sociologist's interest in ethnicity stems not only from a fascination with the variety and complexity of human cultures but also from an interest in social integration. What problems arise when a society like America, for example, takes in such a huge variety of racial and ethnic groups and tries to integrate them into the American Way of Life? The common language and legal system, the general desire to achieve the 'American Dream' of success and a political system that caters for such diversity are obviously crucial in such a social process.

The Sociology of RACE stems primarily from the study of race as a form of social differentiation and the resultant effect on relations between the races of a particular society. It involves the analysis of RACISM — the ideas, attitudes and practices of individuals and society at large that lead to one racial group suffering discrimination, inferiority and inequality in terms of opportunities and life-chances in comparison with or at the hands of another — both today and in the past. The word 'racism' was introduced in the 1930s to refer to doctrines of racial superiority that were very popular at that time in countries like Nazi Germany.

Examples of racial inequality and oppression have as long a history as that of slavery and numerous theories have been advanced to justify the superiority of one race over another. In the eighteenth and nineteenth centures, British colonists talked of the 'White Man's Burden' as they conquered and civilised the 'backward' tribes of Africa, for instance. Others used theories of Social Darwinism, that whites were intellectually and socially more advanced than the 'natives'. Sociologists generally reject such biological explanations and see racial inequality as primarily a form of social stratification that both reinforces and cuts across other social divisions such as class and gender. As one delegate to a recent Labour Party Conference (1983) put it, 'I am at the bottom of the pile – I am working-class, a woman and black'.

1 Marxist writers tend to see race as essentially like gender, another form of CLASS rule with similar roots in the economic inequalities and ownership of private property endemic in modern capitalism. They see the solution to all forms of inequality and exploitation as a socialist revolution. Race or colour simply makes such groups more visible and so more vulnerable to class exploitation. Racist ideas, propaganda, prejudices and stereotypes are used by the ruling class to fragment the proletariat, to set white workers against black and so both prevent the development of a common class consciousness and justify the power and privilege of the white elite.

2 Weberian writers like John Rex and David Lockwood, however, see race as distinctly different not only because it cuts across class divisions, uniting middle and working-class blacks in a common cause against white racism but because racism is built into our language, values and consciousness in a way that class is not. Moreover it is important to distinguish between different non-white groups, even black ones, as the cultures, lifestyles and achievements of, say, Asians in Britain differ considerably from those of West Indians.

Whichever approach is adopted, it is also important to distinguish between the different states and experiences of race relations in different countries, comparing, say, the apartheid system of South Africa to the lack of racial conflicts and divisions in countries like Brazil. Britain's experience of race as a domestic issue is a fairly recent one (though we were a major colonial power and heavily involved in the slave trade). It stems from the influx of Asians and West Indians invited into this country just after the Second World War because of a shortage of white workers to do the 'dirty jobs' in our hospitals, transport and cleansing systems. Grossly exaggerated fears that this country was about to be 'swamped' have led to the present strict immigration laws. In fact only 2.2 million people in Britain today are from the New Commonwealth and Pakistan (OPCS 1983). Most of our immigrants are white and more people leave Britain today than come in.

Within Britain, studies by sociologists and the various race relations bodies have shown that racial discrimination in terms of pay, housing, education, health and the like is not just a matter of isolated examples of prejudice but is virtually INSTITUTIONALISED – built into the way our major social institutions operate – the police, schools, housing departments, etc.

Thus as Castles and Kosack (*Immigrant Workers and Class Structure in Western Europe*, 1973) argued, not only do blacks suffer the inequalities of the unskilled working class but they are doubly disadvantaged by suffering racial discrimination, getting worse pay, jobs and housing than whites of similar qualifications and aptitudes. They feel that their treatment by the police, the courts, politicians and the media is distinctly different and highly stereotyped. The sense of stigma and rejection is enhanced by racial abuse from, and harassment by such organisations as the National Front and by the constant threat of repatriation. Such groups often withdraw into 'ghettos', develop a siege mentality and/or radical ideas such as those of Rastafarians or Black Power. The riots of 1981 were therefore not surprising; what was surprising was the limited number of them and their lack of racial overtones. Ken Pryce's book *Endless Pressure* (1979) is an excellent view from the inside of one riot area (St Paul's, Bristol), delineating it as to the way black people experience our society and adapt to it. But are legal attempts to overcome racial discrimination as in the 1965 Race Relations Act enough? Is it so built into our consciousness and institutions that white people too need 'liberating' from racism?

See also CLASS, STATUS, GENDER, LABELLING, STEREOTYPE.

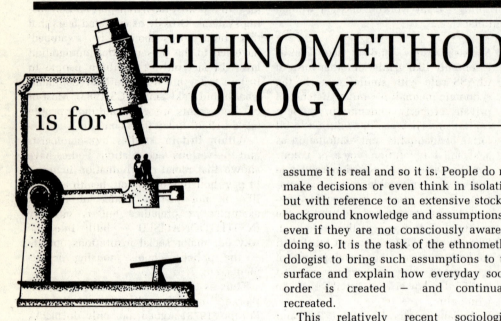

ETHNOMETHOD-OLOGY

is for

assume it is real and so it is. People do not make decisions or even think in isolation but with reference to an extensive stock of background knowledge and assumptions — even if they are not consciously aware of doing so. It is the task of the ethnomethodologist to bring such assumptions to the surface and explain how everyday social order is created — and continually recreated.

This relatively recent sociological approach stems primarily from the work of the American sociologist Harold Garfinkel. From a study of jurors he noticed that their apparently rational decisions were in fact based almost subconsciously on a store of background knowledge about the way society worked and how a jury ought to act. In a subsequent experiment he got a group of students with personal problems to consult an apparently professional therapist. Even though this fake therapist gave only 'yes' and 'no' answers, entirely at random and couldn't be seen by the students, they came away satisfied be-

Ethnomethodology means literally 'the study of the methods employed by members of society' to make sense of their society, their daily lives and of the world about them. Whilst most sociologists take SOCIAL ORDER for granted, ethnomethodologists have made the study of everyday order, routines and 'common sense' the very heart of their sociological analyses. Our everyday social world may appear to be intrinsically structured, may seem to really exist, but that, argue ethnomethodologists, is only a surface impression created by people's everyday interactions — they

cause they had 'made sense' of his answers by imposing some sort of order on them and relating them to the problem involved. In other experiments to highlight the assumptions and expectations behind the order of everyday life, Garfinkel got his students to act as lodgers in their own homes and to ask old ladies and pregnant women to give up their seats on buses. The chaos that resulted showed just how much we take order and routine for granted.

Three key and interrelated concepts in this approach are the DOCUMENTARY METHOD, INDEXICALITY and REFLEX-IVITY. The DOCUMENTARY Method, argues Garfinkel, is the way members of society make sense of the social world and give it a semblance of order by selecting, defining and interpreting any given event or occasion as an example or DOCUMENT of a broader set of events, which in turn are used to make sense of the specific. Each provides evidence of and so supports the other. This INDEXICALITY means that no action or situation makes sense without reference to its context — 'each is used to elaborate the other'. Such circular interpretation from the particular to the general and back again is REFLEXIVE and through this process members of society not only make sense of their 'world', they CREATE and RECREATE it. Occasionally misunderstandings arise, and so to successfully accomplish a common understanding of a particular situation, those involved have to REPAIR indexicality. For example in his study of coroners (*Discovering Suicide*, 1978) Maxwell J. Atkinson showed how, in a sense, such officials 'create' the facts and figures on suicide by the way they look for, select and interpret certain clues as evidence of self-death. Without the victim's own views and motivations, the coroner has to recreate the scene of death but he doesn't do so randomly but according to an underlying theory of why and how people kill themselves. Such 'background knowledge' is used as the basis of both selecting and interpreting certain clues (a suicide note, a locked door, an unstable back-ground) and rejecting others. Such evidence is made sense of by this background theory and in turn provides support for it. The theories and analyses of other experts — the police, sociologists — rest on the official statistics of suicide which in a sense coroners 'create' by the categories they use and the decisions they make.

Aaron Cicourel (*The Social Organisation of Juvenile Justice*, 1976) similarly showed that the official statistics on crime and delinquency are 'created' by the categorisations used by the police. Using an underlying theory that certain types of youngster are more typically criminal than others and using 'evidence' of this, such as leather jackets, weird hairstyles and a lack of respect, the police tend to concentrate on such groups more than others. So such groups are more likely to end up in the official statistics and be the basis of expert opinions and theories of criminality. Studies like these reveal the highly SUBJECTIVE nature of our social world and the danger of taking even official facts for granted. They show the highly interrelated nature of 'evidence', context and 'commonsense' assumptions, the importance of the setting within which social interaction takes place and, more recently, how crucial language and conversation are in creating social understanding and meaning.

Ethnomethodology is thus in a sense both a phenomenological perspective (see p. 75) and a scientific one. It sees man as creating his own social world and yet has sought to put the minutiae, 'the atoms and molecules' of social life and structure under the sociological microscope by both description and experiments. It is a serious critique of most other sociological perspectives, for:

1 taking the order and reality of social life for granted and without question
2 seeing man as a 'cultural dope', a puppet of external social forces rather than an intelligent and active agent capable of controlling his own world ▶

3 believing that sociologists can be detached observers, capable of truly objective analysis. In the view of ethnomethodologists, like everyone else sociologists operate against a background of assumptions and expectations and so have no special claim, no more 'real' understanding of social reality than anyone else. Hence the concentration of ethnomethodological studies on description rather than theories, even to the point of highly detailed depiction of not only context but the researcher's own impressions and feelings whilst observing others.

Inevitably ethnomethodology has itself been subjected to considerable criticism:

(a) Their small-scale studies of ordinary and routine everyday activities seem to many sociologists boring, trivial and extremely time-consuming, leading nowhere and providing no real basis for grand theories of how society works.

(b) Their picture of the social world seems almost like a mirage, a creation of the people involved in a particular situation. There is a lack of reference to broader social structures, in particular to POWER, to the ability of some groups to control society, to impose their view of reality on others.

(c) Their own view of the subjective nature of sociological analysis means that their descriptions are no better, no more real than anyone else's.

Though this approach no longer has the prominence it did in the early 1970s and despite the immense practical problems involved in such an 'archaeological' method of research, it has highlighted the taken-for-granted assumptions underlying both social reality and many other sociological perspectives and the subjective influences behind even such objective facts as official statistics.

See also FUNCTIONALISM, INTERACTIONISM, MARXISM (as comparative sociological perspectives); PHENOMENOLOGY AND POSITIVISM

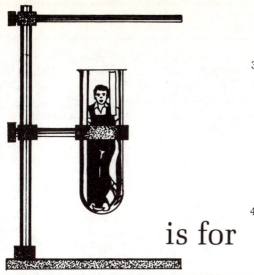

E is for EXPERIMENT

This is the classic research technique of the natural sciences. In the laboratory the scientist can in theory identify, measure and control every factor, accurately analyse the cause-and-effect relationship of the variables involved and so produce theories that can predict future events. Other scientists can repeat these experiments exactly and recheck the results, so verifying conclusions that may further scientific knowledge and help reveal the laws of nature.

Experiments in the social sciences, however, are much more difficult:

1 Their subject matter does not consist of inanimate objects such as rocks and soil but human beings who have minds of their own. Humans are unlikely to act naturally in an experimental situation because they recognise it for what it is and may be influenced by the presence of the researcher.

2 It is rarely possible to get a representative sample of people, willing to be the subject of experiments. The most common of human 'guinea pigs' — students and prisoners — are hardly representative of the population at large.

3 Experiments on human beings raise all sorts of ethical questions. You cannot, in a free society, force people to agree to be experimented on. The experiment's effects cannot always be predicted and it may have a lifelong effect on the people involved. If the social scientist tricks people into an experimental situation, people's trust in scientists is likely to disappear.

4 The alternative of studying people in their natural environment (at home, at work) rather than in the laboratory, raises its own problems. It is even more difficult to control the situation, to identify and analyse every factor involved and determine which are 'causes', which 'effects'. It is almost impossible to recreate a 'natural' situation. Those involved now know what is going to happen and so act differently, inevitably producing different results to the original experiment.

5 Social factors are less easy to analyse than physical ones. Whilst a chemical can be broken down precisely into its constituent parts, social concepts like 'class' cover a wide range of influences from family size to parental encouragement, each of indeterminate importance. The social scientist has no microscope or dissecting knife to analyse his subject-matter in minute detail, section by section.

6 Social processes and relationships take place over too long a period of time to be conducive to 'experimental' analysis.

7 Whilst the natural scientist is unlikely to influence his subject matter, the social scientist may have what is called an 'Experimenter Effect'. People's behaviour often changes, when they are being observed. Humans react to the person studying them, however detached the researcher may try to be. A different ▶

researcher of a different sex or colour, with a warmer personality may well produce a different reaction and so different results.

8 Finally, no human studying other humans can be totally unbiased and impartial. Inevitably his own cultural background and values influence both the way the researcher studies other people and the conclusions reached, however objective he or she may try to be (see OBJECTIVITY, p. 69.)

Social scientists such as psychologists, interested mainly in individual or small-group behaviour, have tried to overcome some of these problems by using, for example, two-way mirrors. However, for sociologists, interested primarily in group behaviour in 'natural' situations, the experiment is of limited use.

Some attempts have been made at QUASI-EXPERIMENTS using control groups. For example, to test a new teaching technique, two 'matched' groups of pupils may be chosen, one taught in the 'traditional' style, the other using a new method, and the test results of the two groups compared afterwards to see which method was the more effective.

However, for most sociologists, the problems of the experimental method outweigh the advantages, and so they have turned to various statistical techniques for analysing surveys, measuring errors and producing predictions OR they have rejected the whole 'scientific' approach to sociological analysis in favour of techniques like participant observation. The fieldwork of ethnomethodologists like Harold Garfinkel in the 1970s, led to some revival of 'natural' experiments. To highlight the taken-for-granted assumptions and the rules governing our everyday routines, he would get his students to disrupt normal daily life, by acting as lodgers in their own homes or asking old ladies to give up their seats on buses. (See p. 34.) Overall, though, whilst the EXPERIMENT is of limited value to the sociologist, the general approach of SCIENTIFIC METHOD or HYPOTHESIS testing and verification still has a profound influence.

See also HYPOTHESIS, POSITIVISM, OBJECTIVITY.

is for
FEUDALISM

Feudalism was the main form of SOCIAL STRATIFICATION in medieval Europe. It was a system based primarily on land, the chief source of wealth in agrarian society; and it involved a hierarchy of authority, rights and power from the highest, the king, to the lowest, the serf. Thus everyone knew his place — and was kept in it — to ensure the agricultural system worked properly, and to try and keep some form of law and order in the era of constant warring between rival barons and monarchs.

The feudal hierarchy in medieval England consisted of royalty; nobility; lesser gentry; free tenants; villeins; cotters; serfs. The most powerful barons and generals accepted the authority of the existing monarch in return for certain territories, which they sub-divided between their chief lieutenants, and so on down. In return they swore allegiance to the king, agreed to maintain law and order and to supply him with armed men and money. Such territories were called FIEFS and could be passed on to the eldest son. Every holder of a fief was a tenant of the person above him — one man's Lord was another man's VASSAL. Thus feudal societies in Europe were covered by an intricate network of duties and obligations linking the highest and the lowest in society — a sort of pyramid with the king at the top. The key economic level in this highly decentralised system of agriculture was the MANOR. All the peasants and serfs of the village had to work for or pay tithes to the lord of the manor, in return for which they gained some protection and the right to farm their own strips of land and to wood and water on the common land.

This rigid hierarchy was reinforced by the church, often the most wealthy of landowners, and prepared to use its powers of excommunication against those who rebelled against the king.

The feudal system is often referred to as the ESTATE system, with the nobility and clergy forming the first two estates — the nobility provided the soldiers, administrators and magistrates; the clergy provided for the people's spiritual and moral welfare. However, from the thirteenth century onwards simple feudalism began to decline with the growth of trade, industry, towns and the rise of the professional classes. With industrialisation, the feudal system of social stratification was gradually replaced by one based on occupation, skills and business wealth — our present class system of middle and working class. Yet even today we have remnants of feudalism in modern Britain — our monarchy and the House of Lords, for instance.

Feudalism offers a good contrast to our more open and flexible CLASS system of social stratification (see p. 13). It was a strict and clearly defined system of stratification. Everyone knew his place and the duties that went with it. A class system is far less rigid and less easy to define.

It was a relatively 'closed' system. There was little SOCIAL MOBILITY (see p. 104). If you were born a serf, you could never ▶

become a noble. The only avenue of mobility was the Church – the rise of Cardinal Wolsey to become Henry VIII's Chancellor was an example of this. Advanced industrial societies seem in comparison very open. Anyone who has talent and ambition seems to have the opportunity to rise up the social scale – though as studies like John Goldthorpe *et al*'s recent work (*Social Mobility and Class Structure in Modern Britain*, 1980) show, even here, mobility is not as great as is often supposed.

Marxist writers see the feudal mode of production as a typical example of class exploitation and oppression by which the king and his nobles enjoyed a high standard of living and great privilege by forcibly extracting their agricultural surplus from the peasantry. However, as is not the case in capitalism, where the workers own no property save their own labour, the peasants did own their own land. The lord of the manor simply took rent, or rent in kind, from them. This class conflict eventually led to the French Revolution and other European uprisings in the eighteenth and nineteenth centuries by which the feudal system based on land gave way to the capitalist system based on industry and trade, and the rule of the king and aristocracy gave way to the government of businessmen and merchants.

See also CASTE, CLASS, GENDER, ETHNICITY.

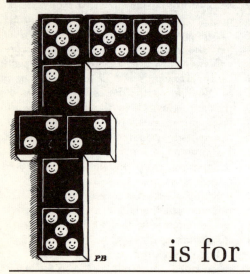

is for

FUNCTIONALISM

back to the upheavals of the political and industrial revolutions of the eighteenth and nineteenth centuries, when such founding fathers of sociology as Comte, Spencer and Durkheim sought to analyse social order by adopting a scientific approach, based on the view that:

1 People are naturally selfish and require strict control.
2 Society has a life of its own, above and beyond the sum of its members. Even apparently individual acts such as suicide can best be explained as social facts·that vary from society to society.
3 Society is best analysed as a system with many interrelated parts, all

Functionalism is one of the main approaches developed by sociologists to explain social behaviour. It can be traced functioning on the basis of a consensus about basic values towards specific goals, particularly survival.

This 'perspective concentrates on analysing the sources of social harmony and balance. The usual analogy is that of a biological organism. For example, the human body comprises many interrelated parts, all functioning in harmony for the general health of the whole. Individuals can be likened to the cells of a body: they may die but the body will continue. Thus any social institution, value, group or form of behaviour, can best be analysed in terms of its function, its contribution towards a society's stability and the achievement of its goals. Other functionalist writers have used a mechanical or a systems analogy. Malinowski, an anthropologist, outlined such social goals as the human need for food, shelter, sexual satisfaction, protection, etc. Radcliffe-Brown went on to analyse the social structures that have arisen to fulfil such goals. For example, the economic system produces required goods and services, the political system makes decisions and allocates resources, and the cultural system (religion, the mass media and so on) organises society's values.

The most sophisticated explanation of functionalism has been that of the American sociologist, Talcott Parsons. He concentrated on the social system – the way it keeps itself in balance, and maintains certain boundaries with its environment. Just as a human body has to adapt to its environment (it perspires in heat) so a society has to adapt to the resources it has available (the physical system). It has to ensure harmony amongst its members in pursuing its goals (the cultural system), and it has to socialise its members into the various roles required for social order and goal-attainment (the personality system).

Functionalism thus explains social behaviour in terms of the needs of society rather than according to individual motives. People are seen as being moulded and conditioned into fulfilling society's needs. Through our families, friends, schools and so on, we learn the norms and roles required by our society. Our economic system provides us with food and clothing:

our political system makes decisions for us in time of war, many of us will die so our society can survive.

The strength and popularity of functionalism has been its claim to be scientific, capable of determining the regularities of social order and behaviour. Moreover, it offered a purely sociological explanation of human behaviour as distinct from the traditional ones based on psychology, biology or religion. However, in recent years this perspective has been severely criticised:

1   Phenomenologists in particular attack its deterministic view of man. They oppose the view of human behaviour being simply the result of external forces in the way natural elements (say, rocks or trees) are. Rather, they say, men have minds of their own and are capable of controlling their own futures. By relying solely on OBSERVABLE behaviour, this approach is unable to analyse motives, feelings and emotions. It sees such SUBJECTIVE factors as irrelevant to scientific analysis. It concentrates on HOW people behave, not WHY.

2   It overemphasises social consensus. Advanced industrial societies are far too complex and heterogeneous to be explained in terms of a few simple goals and values.

3   It overemphasises social order and stability and fails to explain social change, especially revolutionary upheavals. In his analyse of deviance and bureaucracy Robert K. Merton sought to overcome such criticisms by distinguishing between MANIFEST and LATENT functions (intended and unintended) and developing the concept of DYSFUNCTIONS (when a social item or institution hinders or obstructs social harmony and goal achievement). Lewis Coser's analyses of social conflict had a similar purpose, seeing such conflict as an integrating force promoting competition and efficiency. Essentially, ▶

FUNCTIONALISM (continued)

however, there is no mechanism in functionalist theory for explaining social change in the way that, say, Marx's 'class struggle' does.

4   It is very conservative approach. It not only explains the existing social order but seems to justify it: to see it as the best system simply because it exists and functions. It thus fails to provide any basis for criticising or reforming a particular social order. It is TELEOLOGICAL, trying to explain the existence of a social activity by its consequences. Nevertheless it is still one of the major sociological perspectives and even under attack, has stimulated such alternative theories as the 'conflict' and 'social action' approaches.

See also INTERACTIONISM, MARXISM, POSITIVISM.

is for
GENDER

Whilst the term 'sex' is used by sociologists to refer to biological differences between men and women, the term 'gender' is used to refer to social and cultural differences in their behaviour and social roles.

The Sociology of Gender debates such issues as the extent to which the 'traditional' roles of men (as warriors, breadwinners and decision-makers) and of women (in the home, looking after children) are natural and inevitable or social, and so changeable. Similarly, are the ways of behaving we call masculinity and femininity solely reflections of innate genetic differences? Is male dominance of the home and society at large inevitable? Why does the fact of being born male or female have such a crucial influence not only on personality and identity but on behaviour, lifestyle and lifechances?

Such questions are part of the broader nature-nurture debate as to the key determinants of human behaviour and intelligence (see SOCIALISATION, p. 107). Over the years the Naturist case has been based on a wide variety of innate biological factors – physical strength, instinct, genetic make-up, biogrammars, psychological needs – in its attempt to show that men are naturally the superior sex and that the traditional division of sexual labour is both functional and fulfilling. Nurturists have replied by citing examples of women doing men's jobs (bricklaying in Soviet Russia, fighting in Vietnam) and equalling men's feats (as in long-distance swimming). Writers like Margaret Mead and Ann Oakley have cited examples of societies where the traditional sex roles are reversed (the Tchambuli tribe of New Guinea) or at least equally shared (the Mbuti Pygmies of the Congo).

In a massive review of the 'scientific' research on sex differences Eleanor Maccoby and Carol Jacklin (*The Psychology of Sex Differences*, 1974) concluded that though certain differences did exist, as in the superiority of boys in visual spatial tests or of girls in verbal skills, they were insufficient to explain the huge social differences in the two sexes' achievements or even personalities (the aggression of boys, the emotionality of girls). If then social factors also have an important influence, how do they operate? Sociologists in this field, primarily feminists, have identified two key and related factors:

1   SOCIALISATION: We tend to bring children up to be boys and girls rather than individuals, by dressing them differently (dresses and trousers) giving them different toys (dolls and guns) and responding to them very differently ('big' boys don't cry but little girls can), as we prepare them for future roles as mothers and fathers. According to studies such as Sue Sharpes, *Just Like a Girl* and Mary K. Benet, *Secretary*, such sex-role stereotyping is continued by school and work and reinforced by the media (portraying women in the kitchen or on page 3 of a tabloid newspaper).

2   PATRIARCHY: a structure of power by which men rule women virtually as a class. Such a form of social stratification is based not only on male dominance of all the top institutions in our society but on an all-pervasive ideology of male superiority. Male dominance is accepted even by women as natural and normal and so is largely unquestioned. Though today women in advanced societies like Britain and America seem to have far greater freedom and many more rights than ever before (the vote, equal pay and job opportunity legislation, reformed divorce and property laws) they still do not enjoy true equality with men. For example, though over 40% of the British workforce is female, women are concentrated in 'women's' work (nursing, teaching, typing), working for men for less pay than their male counterparts. Few women are in such 'masculine' occupations as engineering, and fewer

still reach the top of even 'female' professions.

Part of the reason, according to some surveys, is a bias by employers (mainly male) against employing and promoting women. Though girls' O and A level results are now as good as boys' (*Social Trends 1984*), they tend to be mainly in 'feminine' subjects such as English and languages and only a third of first-year university graduates are girls. Despite Mrs Thatcher's election as Britain's first woman prime minister, only 23 out of the present 650 MPs are women.

The cornerstone of patriarchy, argue feminists, is the family and marriage which bind women to housework and child-rearing, to low status, no pay, invisibility and a lack of independence and self-expression. Feminism has tried to highlight and understand such inequalities. Women's Liberationists have tried to raise the consciousness of women as a 'class' to their subordination and oppression inside and outside the home. Feminism can be broadly divided into two main schools of thought:

(a) Socialist or Marxist feminism which sees the position of women today as part of the general exploitation and sense of private property of modern capitalism. As housewives and mothers, women keep male workers fit and healthy and reproduce workers of the future; as workers themselves women provide a reserve army of cheap labour employers can draw on when faced by a shortage of workers or which can be used to break men's demands for higher pay. Male dominance at home provides some psychological outlet for their powerlessness at work. Thus female oppression is seen simply as another form of class exploitation; 'come the revolution' women too will be liberated.

(b) Radical or revolutionary feminists are not so optimistic because even in so called socialist societies, women still tend to take second place. They see patriarchy as the oldest form of social stratification and ▶

GENDER (continued)

possibly biological in basis and so highly unlikely to 'wither away' simply through a change in the economic structure. Male violence and aggression as expressed in wifebattering, rape and pornography, in their view, is almost innate and so some such feminists advocate a total separation of women from men, a sort of 'sexual apartheid' whilst others like Schulasmith Firestone (*The Dialectic of Sex*, 1972) believe that only with biological engineering liberating women from their reproductive role, will women ever be truly free and equal.

Feminism has had a tremendous effect on academic thinking, forcing a radical re-analysis of virtually every field of social thinking. It has brought to the surface the unquestioned acceptance of the history of human ideas and achievements being overwhelmingly that of men's ideas and deeds, highlighted the previously 'invisible' contribution of women and revealed the innate 'sexism' in such areas as the school curriculum and even everyday language.

The Sociology of Gender, however, also has a 'masculine' perspective. A true sexual revolution, argue feminists, must also involve the liberation of men – from their traditional roles as dominators and from masculine stereotypes where strength and aggression are expected and sensitivity frowned upon. The mass unemployment of the 1980s has led a number of husbands to swop roles, to take over at least some responsibility for the home and children whilst their wives go to work.

The Sociology of Gender has also brought to light those groups and individuals who do not neatly fit traditional heterosexual stereotypes – homosexuals, lesbians, trans-sexuals – and so has given support to the Gay Liberation Movements, demands for greater freedom of sexual expression and identity. Examples like the Xaniths of Oman have provided evidence for the possibility of a Third Sex, people who are biologically men but act like women and are accepted by their societies as such.

The Sociology of Gender has therefore led to a dramatic re-examination not only of our traditional ideas about male/female roles, masculinity and femininity but the extent to which the existing structure of power and even knowledge is sexually biased, a reflection of both male and heterosexual dominance.

Would female rule (matriarchy) have produced a more caring world with less war and aggression? Is true sexual equality for all, only possible in an ANDROGYNOUS society where gender is no longer a primary source of personal and social identification? How far do schools help steer girls towards marriage rather than careers and ambition (consider whether in your own school certain subjects are 'labelled' boys' or 'girls' and why; whether boys get or demand more attention from teachers; why there are so few women scientists and mathematicians; why there are so few women in top positions in schools and how this affects girls' attitudes and aspirations).

See also CLASS, ETHNICITY/RACE, LABELLING, SOCIALISATION, STEREOTYPE.

is for
GROUPS

GROUP is not one of the more specialised sociological terms. Nevertheless, it is one of central importance to all the social sciences in their search for the social factors governing human behaviour. People have to cooperate with others in order to survive, to give their lives direction and meaning. They need various kinds of relationships with others; so they can join a wide variety of social groups. Some last a lifetime, such as the family. Some are more temporary, such as a youth club. But they all influence our behaviour in one way or another.

A group can be said to exist when a number of individuals, who have similar interests or attitudes in common, combine together for a certain purpose — informally or in an organised structure. For a group to

fulfil its objectives, maintain its common interests or even survive, it has to ensure that all its members conform to certain basic rules or NORMS, based usually on habit, tradition, agreement, culture, and most of all, the expectations of others (ROLES, see p. 92).

In most families the husband is expected to be the breadwinner, the wife the home-maker; but through agreement such expectations can change — for example, the husband takes over the housework. In a less traditional group, people conform because they want to be respected, accepted by, and popular with others. Those who go against the group norms are soon isolated and socially pressured by, say, 'being sent to Coventry'. The 'school swot' has always been a figure of fun.

Equally, such 'deviants' provide opportunities for re-affirming group unity (Durkheim). Even within deviant or drop-out groups, such as criminals or junkies, there are strong pressures to conform to their norms, however anti-social these may be.

Sociologists have distinguished between PRIMARY and SECONDARY groups, a distinction which refers to the quality of the relationships involved. Members of a primary group have a strong feeling of belonging to the group as a whole. They have face-to-face relationships, enjoy a strong sense of solidarity and represent the social and moral foundations of society at large.

The family represents the major primary group. Secondary groups are based more on some form of contractual relationship — as in a factory, school or hospital. Or they are larger collections of people which display some sort of unity and common interaction, such as social classes.

Sociologists such as Robert K. Merton have gone on to talk about REFERENCE GROUPS, groups that individuals use as a means of self-evaluation or to aspire to and model their behaviour and values on, in the hope of thus gaining acceptance. Such a concept has been used in studies of ▶

GROUPS (continued)

'working-class Tories', and of relative deprivation. Max Weber developed the idea of STATUS GROUPS (see p. 109) as an important form of social stratification.

Research into small groups particularly in the 1950s and 1960s, developed into a speciality of its own, based on the work of C. H. Cooley and George Simmel. This socio-psychological analysis of group dynamics gained particular attention with S. A. Stouffer's study *The American Soldier*, an analysis of morale and efficiency amongst Allied troops in the Second World War. Other notable studies from this school included Kurt Lewin's study of leadership patterns and group interaction amongst young children (an analysis of the relative efficiency in terms of group cohesion, morale and effectiveness of authoritarian, *laissez-faire* and democratic forms of leadership) and the Tavistock Institute of Human Relations Studies on group behaviour in the workplace.

However, can such micro-studies really explain group behaviour in society at large where the individual is faced by a multitude of conflicting pressures? The PLURALIST analyses of Robert Dahl and Arnold Rose were one attempt to develop this (see p. 28); INTERACTIONIST studies were another (see p. 52). Thus despite its rather mundane, everyday origins, the Group is a key concept in modern sociology.

See also INTERACTIONISM, PEER GROUP.

is for
HYPOTHESIS

Before a sociologist investigates any aspect of society or social behaviour, he usually has some idea or theory in mind. Such a HYPOTHESIS must be empirical — that is, testable — not just an idea which it would be impossible to do research into, such as the existence of God.

Bearing in mind his own knowledge of existing theories about social behaviour the sociologist puts forward a hypothesis about, say, voting behaviour. The next step is to do research to prove or disprove the idea via, say, a social survey. If the hypothesis is proved correct it may provide enough support for the sociologist's general theory on voting behaviour, to be considered a LAW within the social sciences.

But if research proves the hypothesis false, the sociologist must go back to the drawing board and consider whether his statement was badly constructed, his research inadequate, or his basic theory at fault. Usually, however, hypotheses are neither completely confirmed nor totally rejected, but, rather, proved partially true. This means that the original theory must be modified.

Such a process of what Sir Karl Popper called 'conjecture and refutation' forms the basis of SCIENTIFIC METHOD. This series of steps (observation, conjecture, hypothesis formation, testing, control, generalisation, theory formation, all based on OBJECTIVITY) is what distinguishes SCIENCE from non-scientific approaches. Scientists, natural or social, put forward new ideas and conjectures which they and the rest of the scientific community then try to refute. If they cannot do so, such hypotheses form the basis of scientific theories. Scientific theories are therefore never proven, merely so far unrefuted.

Generally the whole process is much more haphazard than this. Through reading or discussion, some vague idea about possible causal relationships between, say, suicide rates and industrial development germinates in the sociologist's mind. On reading the relevant literature, he finds no one has tackled the problem from this angle. So he sets up a research project to collect data (information) which he carefully analyses. The results are published so that other sociologists can evaluate and reanalyse his work and highlight its deficiencies. If his results prove to be sound, and are well received by fellow academics, the sociologist may go on to refine his hypothesis in other areas of human behaviour in an attempt to construct a general theory.

The obvious problem about this kind of research, is that the researcher only collects evidence to support his own hypothesis and ignores any against it. The scientific approach demands impartiality and as far as possible the avoidance of bias ▶

HYPOTHESIS (continued)

and prejudice. Many sociologists, however, feel that unlike the natural sciences, the investigation of human behaviour can never really be value-free, since the researcher is himself human and so inevitably is influenced by his own values and preferences.

In the view of PHENOMENOLOGISTS, social investigators should not try to suppress their human instincts, but to use them positively to gain scientific insights into why people act the way they do. Human behaviour, they feel, is too complex to be reduced to simple 'cause and effect' statements, as the scientific POSITIVIST approach demands.

For example, the behaviour of a class of pupils will change if, say, a teacher enters the room or if they are aware of being watched by a researcher; the behaviour or composition of a geological sample will not change, whoever is watching it. Such sociologists regard hypothesis as more of an impediment than a help, since their aim, through their own human understanding, is to try to see a situation in the same way as those involved in it. Such an INTERPRETATIVE approach prefers participant observation to social surveys as a research technique.

See also EXPERIMENT, POSITIVISM.

is for
IDEAL TYPES

A big problem for social scientists, compared with their colleagues in the natural sciences, is that they have to deal with thinking, feeling people, not inanimate objects. The natural scientist can obtain pure chemicals or gases for experiments, but the social scientist cannot obtain 'pure' people. One way this can be overcome is by the use of IDEAL TYPES, which do not really exist, but which provide a standard against which the subject being studied can be judged. Complex reality can thus be broken down and analysed more simply. You could, for instance, construct an ideal-type teacher against which to judge or compare actual teachers, and so establish guidelines for improvement.

An important proponent of this technique was Max Weber. In his analysis of the influence of Protestantism on western capitalism, he could not possibly take a random sample of all Protestants in history. Instead he had to use typical examples – John Wesley, the founder of Methodism was one. Similarly, his typical capitalist was something of a caricature – but how else could he attempt to test the interrelationships of capitalism and the Protestant ethnic? Weber's conclusion allowed for the weakness of his method by claiming that Protestantism merely stimulated *not* caused industrialisation in Western Europe. A classic example of Weber's Ideal Types was that of BUREAU-CRACY, which he saw as likely to be the main form of organisational structure in advanced industrial societies. (See BUREAUCRACY, p. 6.)

It is important to remember that an ideal type is not ideal in any ethical sense. The sociologist is not claiming that his ideal type is the best or most desirable. It should merely be the most logical for his purposes of investigation. Ideal types are different from average types, which are made up of traits common to all aspects of the subject being investigated. Ideal Types are one example of a COMPARATIVE METHOD. Lacking the controlled conditions of a laboratory or the dissective instruments of a natural scientist, social scientists have sought to identify and analyse the key features of a particular society or social institution by means of comparing a variety of societies or social structures. There has never been one simple or dominant 'comparative method' but certain schools of sociological thought have developed their own:

Evolutionary theorists, particularly those of the nineteenth century, sought to apply the concepts and techniques of such natural sciences as biology to social analysis. Thus societies were classified and categorised like plants or animals — by their origins, organisation and life-cycle. They looked for the common roots of a variety of societies and to theories like that of Herbert Spencer, who analysed social evolution in Darwinian terms of survival of the fittest.

Functionalism, particularly that derived from the work of Emile Durkheim, has sought to compare the evolutionary development of various societies at key stages in their growth. In particular, the way key elements in the social structure contribute to the overall functioning, stability and balance of that society. Durkheim's famous study of suicide aimed to scientifically analyse how the integrative structure of different societies created different rates of suicide.

Marxist theories of historical development — based on economic change and class struggle rather than natural evolution — also lend themselves to comparative analysis, enabling such writers to compare the different stages of economic development (or modes of production) of both past and present societies and those today in the First, Third and Communist worlds.

Modern statistical and computer techniques, the abundance of social information and the use of multivariate and regression techniques mean that all manner of social variables can be combined, compared and cross-analysed — from the relationship between class and voting to that between unemployment and crime.

However, such comparative analyses and ideal types have been criticised for taking variables out of their social context, so making them meaningless. So much of a particular country's character or development depends on its own particular social and historical background and culture that to take, say, its education system out in isolation and compare it to another country's can lead to overgeneralisation.

See also EXPERIMENT.

is for
IDEOLOGY

A set of systematically interrelated IDEAS and beliefs about the nature of man, society and government which form a framework or theory about how society is or ought to be organised.

The word itself is said to have been first used by the French cavalry leader and philosopher Destutt de Tracy (1755-1836) in his four-volume book *Eléments d'idéologie*. By ideology he meant a science of ideas, a framework for scientifically analysing theories and beliefs to discover the truth, eliminate errors and eventually provide the basis of a theory of mental processes.

Though amongst professional social scientists and philosophers, the term ideology still has this sort of neutral and unbiased meaning, more generally it has become associated with political and religious creeds based as much on values and emotions as ideas. Such ideologies may be *explicit*, systematically and logically thought-out and clearly expressed – as in, say, a political pamphlet or manifesto or they may be *implicit*, theoretically incomplete and expressed more as emotional slogans and prejudices than a clearly thought-out system of ideas. Both these types of ideology are often more than a set of ideas, they are a guide to future action, a blueprint for creating an ideal society in the future and their followers often have a fervent even fanatical faith in the truth of their particular creed. It is often difficult therefore to scientifically and dispassionately analyse such ideologies. Marxism is an example of an explicit ideology with a systematically constructed set of concepts based on the theoretical analysis of man, society and social change. Conservatism is a more implicit ideology, much more general, often critical of theoretical blueprints and yet held together by certain underlying assumptions about the true nature of man, society and government.

Within sociology, the controversy over whether sociology is or ought to be a science has been a major source of controversy and part of this debate has been a discussion about the extent to which sociology is 'real' knowledge or simply ideology. As outlined in the sections on POSITIVISM (p. 78) and OBJECTIVITY (p. 69), Positivists believe that the social world, like the natural one, has a reality of its own and that by using scientific method and being objective, the sociologist can identify its underlying structure and laws of development and change. Functionalists in particular have sought to establish sociology as a scientific discipline, though it is often seen as a political ideology. Marxism too claims to be a 'science of society' but with a difference. From a Marxist perspective existing knowledge is largely 'bourgeois ideology' covering up rather than exposing the true reality of capitalist society. Alternative perspectives such as functionalism are castigated by Marxists as being ideologically-biased because instead of critically analysing capitalism, they tend to accept it as natural, inevitable or simply the best economic system available. They tend to ignore or underplay the exploitation, gross inequalities and class conflict that underlie market economies and so help justify and defend what Marxists see as an inherently sick and unjust social system. Such bourgeois knowledge helps keep the masses ignorant of their exploitation, in a state of false consciousness.

In the *German Ideology*, for example, Marx and Engels claimed that the dominant ideas of any particular historical period did not reflect reality but the views of that epoch's ruling class.

By getting the masses to accept their view of reality, alternative ideas about a fairer distribution of wealth and power could be dismissed as utopian propaganda, unrealistic or threatening and so 'justifiably' crushed. By controlling people's ideas, such ruling classes were able to preserve and legitimise their privilege and wealth far more effectively than by using force. Whilst in the past religion provided such ideological control, in advanced capitalist society education and the media serve this purpose. Marx and Engels claimed that their 'scientific' analysis of history and society exposed such indoctrination and such false consciousness and so revealed the true nature of class relations, struggle and exploitation. Moreover as a 'scientific' analysis it was able to predict the future, the inevitable progress from capitalism to socialism and communism. Only when a classless society is achieved will ideology be a true reflection of reality.

Karl Mannheim (1893-1947) however used the term 'ideology' in a more specific way in his book *Ideology and Utopia* (1929). He used the term ideology to refer to sets of ideas used to justify the *status quo* and the term Utopian to refer to those arguing for radical social change. He saw ideologies as the beliefs and values of a ruling group which 'obscures the real condition of society both to itself and others and thereby stabilises it'. He saw 'Utopian' ideologies as also obscuring reality but their distortion arose from a vision of the future rather than a defence of the present social system. Utopian ideologies are usually those of oppressed groups aiming to establish a more just society. He saw Marxism as an example of such utopianism whilst functionalism is often cited — especially by radical writers — as an example of a Ruling Class ideology.

The term 'ideology' is therefore a crucial concept not only in the sociologies of politics and religion but in that of knowledge. Positivists — and, as explained above, this includes Marxists — believe that society has a reality of its own that can be discovered in terms of such social 'facts' as crime and class. Phenomenologists do not. In their view all ideas and knowledge have an underlying ideological basis. Even 'facts' are not things in themselves about which there can be no dispute but are socially created, are the result of categories and ideas used by people to make sense of their social worlds. For example there is no such thing as a crime; it all depends on how a particular form of behaviour is viewed in a particular situation. Thus whilst killing someone in peacetime would normally be called murder, in wartime medals are given for such acts of 'heroism'. From such a PHENOMENOLOGICAL perspective all knowledge is RELATIVE, all ideas and so-called 'facts' are based on an underlying, often unconscious and taken-for-granted view of the world. Objectivity, and even absolute TRUTH, are therefore impossible and even society itself is ▶

socially, if not psychologically created. It has no reality of its own in the way the natural world seems to.

Like ideas, it's all in our heads – or at least in the heads of those with the power to control the dominant 'ideology' of our period. Marxists would point to the bourgeoisie, feminists to men, black radicals to whites. Such a RELATIVE analysis of knowledge and even REALITY has been adopted even by some natural scientists.

See also OBJECTIVITY, PHENOMENOLOGY, POSITIVISM.

Until recently most sociologists used perspectives that concentrated on the STRUCTURE of society – the larger elements of which society is composed, such as family, kinship, education and so on. INTERACTIONISM takes the opposite view and concentrates on the individual. This approach is based on the view that people create social life by interacting with each other in small groups.

In reaction to the 'MACRO' theories of sociology Interactionism concentrates on the individual's point of view. It argues that people are not like natural phenomena, controlled by external forces, but are capable of exercising FREE WILL, of being CREATIVE and adaptable. It all depends on how a situation is interpreted, what meaning it has; for example two people sitting in a room may be a meeting, a lesson or a liaison.

Interactionists place particular emphasis on Charles Cooley's concept of the 'LOOKING-GLASS SELF' – the idea that we build up an image of ourselves based on what we think others think of us, and act accordingly. They are interested in how individuals define a given situation through the gestures, appearance and especially language of others. For example, a policeman may interpret long hair as a sign of potential deviancy and treat long-haired individuals accordingly. They in turn react to this treatment and may well give the policeman cause to arrest them – so confirming his original belief about them – a sort of 'self-fulfilling prophecy'

is for

INTERACTIONISM
(more often known as SYMBOLIC INTERACTIONALISM)

Social definitions thus evolve through a process of NEGOTIATION. Similarly though the concept of social ROLES is crucial to such analysis, interactionists do not see them as determining social behaviour in the way that functionalists (see p. 40) do, but rather as guidelines within which the actor can manoeuvre and even create. For example a teacher may act in a friendly or a harsh manner depending not only on his own personality and view of his role but according to the particular class he is dealing with or the context involved. Outside school he may be the friendliest of individuals; in it a real tyrant.

So, in contrast to structuralists' search for 'cause and effect' explanations, interactionists are primarily concerned with MOTIVES AND MEANING − hence the emphasis on SYMBOLS, on communication and on INTERPRETATION.

This form of PHENOMENOLOGICAL analysis derives mainly from the work of George Herbert Mead and Herbert Blumer and can be seen in such theories as that of LABELLING (p. 57) and such techniques as PARTICIPANT OBSERVATION (p. 71). During the 1960s such radical analyses overturned traditional assumptions in such fields as deviancy, gender, education and health.

This individualistic, almost psychological, approach has been criticised, especially by positivist sociologists as:

1   able only to explain small-scale, face-to-face situations, not their general social or historical context. It thus provides no real basis for a grand theory of society.
2   failing to explain how social norms, roles and values originate − one 'offshoot' attempting an analysis of social order and routine and the creation of social reality is ETHNOMETHODOLOGY (p. 34).
3   unable to show the extent to which POWER is a crucial aspect of sociological analysis, in particular the power of certain groups over society at large and over its values, goals and ideas.
4   overestimating human freedom of action and underestimating social constraints. (Possibly this overemphasis reflects the American origins of much of this work.)

Nevertheless this approach has dramatically challenged the traditional positivist and especially functionalist domination of sociology and led to valuable insights and a fresh perspective in a variety of fields.

See also FUNCTIONALISM, MARXISM, PHENOMENOLOGY.

staff.

As the children grow older, they move with their age group from one children's house to another. They know their parents and usually visit them for about two hours after work each day, as well as staying with them on Saturdays and holidays. Thus,

is for KIBBUTZIM

women are freed from traditional maternal roles and children come to consider all their peers as brothers and sisters. After high school, boys and girls live in separate rooms. They are not encouraged to have sexual relationships, but may do so if they wish. A couple wishing to live together simply apply for a double room and there is no compulsory marriage ceremony.

The modern 'nuclear family' in advanced western industrial societies has been widely criticised for its exclusiveness, competitiveness and inner tensions. Writers from Plato to Engels to David Cooper have advocated a more communal form of society than the family. One such attempt is the kibbutz in modern Israel.

Kibbutzim are small agricultural communities, varying in size from 60 to 2000 members. Their aim is to establish economic, social and political equality. Their members work not for themselves or for their own families, but for the benefit of the whole community. All property is communally-owned and the income from farming or light industry is pooled in a common treasury. Food, clothing and other necessities are equally distributed, and all eat in communal kitchens.

Social equality is pursued on two levels — to give women greater equality with men, and to bring children up amid a communal rather than a nuclear structure. Thus, women work alongside men in the fields or factory, and children eat, sleep and spend most of their time in special children's houses under the care of special

From a functional and psychological viewpoint, the kibbutz has 'extended' rather than abolished the family. According to Bruno Bettelheim and his 1964 study *Children of the Dream*, the advantages of this form of family life seem to be that kibbutzim children are secure and rarely suffer from the neglect, quarrelling parents or broken homes found in many western societies. Generally the old are equally secure and well cared-for. However, Betelheim did raise questions about how far women had really escaped their gender roles.

Men are employed primarily in agriculture, construction and other traditional male occupations, while women predominate in catering, teaching and nursing. Men dominate political life, holding 80 per cent of major public offices. Similarly, family life, especially in right-wing kibbutzim, is moving closer to the traditional structure, with mothers spending more time with their children and taking over the cooking, ironing and some washing.

So why is it that even in so ideal a society as the kibbutz, traditional sex roles and inequalities seem to be re-establishing themselves? Are such roles biologically inevitable? Or are social factors at work? Kibbutzim do not exist in isolation, they are part of the wider Israeli society – a capitalist one – and are inevitably influenced by it according to one observer, Yonina Talmon. She goes on to suggest that in the early days the kibbutzim were desperately short of labour, so women had to work in the fields. As the standard of living and the use of technology rose,

women were freer to have children and inevitably this led them to concentrate on child care and the provision of allied services – tasks that left them with little time or energy for physical or administrative work.

Despite its shortcomings the kibbutz has proved a major experiment in social liberation and equality and has inspired many others elsewhere.

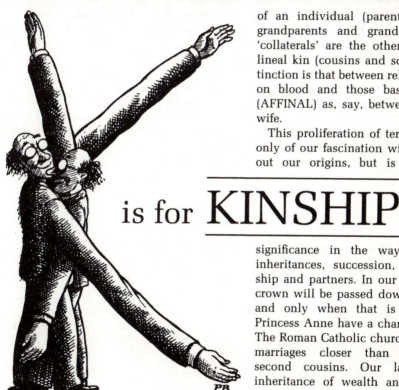

of an individual (parents and children, grandparents and grandchildren), while 'collaterals' are the other descendants of lineal kin (cousins and so on). A key distinction is that between relationships based on blood and those based on marriage (AFFINAL) as, say, between husband and wife.

This proliferation of terms is a sign not only of our fascination with trying to find out our origins, but is of great social

is for KINSHIP

significance in the way we determine inheritances, succession, group membership and partners. In our royal family the crown will be passed down the male line, and only when that is exhausted will Princess Anne have a chance to be Queen. The Roman Catholic church will not allow marriages closer than those between second cousins. Our laws about the inheritance of wealth and property still assume that most of it will go to direct kin.

Kinship refers to the most basic and most sacred of human relationships – those based on 'blood'. Yet, as many a family tree shows, such ties can be extremely complicated – as is much of the terminology surrounding the word. For instance, kin traced through the father are termed 'paternal' or 'patrilineal': those through the mother 'maternal' or 'matrilineal'. Lineal kin are the direct ancestors and descendants

But the most dominant feature of these and all kinship networks is the taboo about 'incest' – the prohibition of sexual relationships between parents and children, sisters and brothers. This is usually based on the fear that such in-breeding may produce biological weaknesses, possibly even madness.

Kinship is therefore the life-blood of any family structure – 'blood is thicker than ▶

KINSHIP (continued)

water' — and so is of immense interest to sociologists trying to explain the great variety found in human social structures.

Quite often simple societies are literally no more than large families themselves. Kinship ties are reinforced by inter-marriage and the family elders are often the tribal chiefs.

In modern societies kin networks are less obvious, and one important controversy between modern sociologists has been the extent to which kin ties have been eliminated by industrialisation and urbanisation. Was Talcott Parsons right in claiming that the extended family network has been replaced by the smaller, more independent nuclear one? Young and Wilmott's researches in East London during the 1950s showed that in traditional working-class areas the 'extended family' was still thriving, though usually based on the declining traditional industries such as dockwork and mining.

Colin Bell's study of middle-class families in Swansea during the 1960s (*Middle Class Families*, 1965), showed that, even among the more mobile families, kin ties were strong — though here the link was often more a financial one, based on the connection between father and son. Nevertheless, industrialisation and urbanisation do seem to have had considerable effects on the nature of kinship. This in turn has led to changes in the structure and functions of the modern family, particularly in the relationship between husbands and wives.

Modern family ties therefore seem as strong as ever but reduced to more immediate family. As Tom Lupton and C.S. Wilson's study 'Top Decision Makers in Britain' (in J. Urry and J. Wakeford (eds), *Power in Britain*, 1983) showed, whilst kin-networks even at this rarified level are very evident they do not necessarily form the basis of a 'ruling elite', rather 'kinship itself may act as a divisive as well as unifying force.' This apt comment can be as true of kin relations between dockers' families as those of top politicians, or even royalty — the kin-network par excellence.

See also SOCIAL ANTHROPOLOGY, POLYGAMY.

is for
LABELLING

family and friends often no longer trust him and fear being tarred with the same brush. Stigmatised and rejected by society, many such people turn back to crime, thus fulfilling suspicions about their being a criminal type – 'a born villain' – a sort of 'self-fulfilling prophecy'.

The essence of labelling theory is, therefore, not so much what the individual does, but the reaction of others. Often the same act of deviance is treated differently – a car theft by a middle-class youth is played down as high spirits, while a working-class youth, especially if black, might be likely to go to Borstal.

Edwin Lemmert has distinguished PRIMARY from SECONDARY deviance – on the one hand, the committing of a deviant act; on the other, the effect on a person's self-image of the reaction of parents, friends and those in authority. In this sense, the labellists are saying the 'cause' of deviancy is often not the action itself, but the reaction of others to it. It is possible, they say, that social control, far from preventing crime, can help cause it. Labellists have also outlined the various stages in a DEVIANT CAREER, the ways in which deviants are in a sense 'created' and processed. Thus whilst Aaron Cicourel has described the features used to identify a potential delinquent by the policeman on the beat – long hair, weird clothes and in particular a disrespectful manner, Erving Goffmann has outlined the processes used by such TOTAL institutions as prisons to transform inmates' self-images, to 'mortify' them by taking away all vestiges of individuality (their personal belongings and clothes, strict haircuts) and of privacy. Stigmatised in this fashion, many individuals come to see themselves as criminal and, reinforced by such inmade ▶

Labelling is one of the most basic aspects of human understanding. Just as we label things – trees, houses, animals – so we tend to label people. We do this in order to simplify our social world – but such labels can equally lead to misunderstanding and confusion.

So common is this social labelling that some sociologists have developed it into a theory. Howard Becker, for example, believed that there is no such thing as a deviant act – it is merely behaviour that other people so label. The important point here is who does the labelling. INFORMAL labelling goes on all the time – every school has its own swot, for example – but FORMAL social labels can only be applied by those in authority. Only a doctor can declare someone sick; only a court can declare a suspect a criminal.

Certain MASTER labels, such as being declared a homosexual, criminal or lunatic, tend to override all others and, once applied, are very difficult to live down. An ex-prisoner, though he has served his sentence, will find it difficult to get a job and settle back into normal life. Employers,

LABELLING (continued)

sub-cultures, live up to this label – some even become institutionalised, fearful of outside society.

Such an analysis has its roots in symbolic interactionism (see p. 52) and phenomenology. It was very popular in the 1950s and 1960s as part of a general critique of positivist criminology which tended to analyse crime solely in terms of criminals. Labelling theory redirected attention from the individual as the cause of crime to the social processes behind definitions of crime and within such social control institutions as the police, courts and prisons.

However, many criticisms have been made of this approach:

1 It fails to explain people's actions BEFORE being labelled. Why do some people commit crime while others do not?
2 It depicts people as too passive. People seem to be minding their own business 'when wham, bad society comes along and stops them with a stigmatizing label': (Ronald Akers, quoted in Gibbons and Jones, *The Study of Deviance*, 1975). Most deviants are in fact well aware of their deviance. They simply hope to avoid detection or are just being defiant.
3 It puts too much emphasis on societal reaction and fails to explain where the agents of social control get their images of deviants from, or why they label some individuals and not others.
4 It fails to explain the basis for authorities like doctors, judges and the police being able to label people.

Marxists in particular criticise the failure of this theory to explain who has the POWER to label and why. In their view the power to label is an important part of the bourgeoisie's social and especially ideological control. By labelling those who threaten its power and privilege as deviants, it can neutralise them. Consider, for example, the labelling by the media of radical critics of Mrs Thatcher's government and of the social system, (such as Tony Benn and Arthur Scargill) as MILITANTS and MARXISTS.

Nevertheless this theory has offered invaluable insights into the processes and effects of labelling people 'deviant', not only in the field of crime but elsewhere. For example, David Hargreaves' work has shown the effect of the labelling of pupils in schools especially when reinforced by streaming whilst feminist writers see the labelling of women as wives and mothers as part of the means for keeping them in the home.

See also DEVIANCE, STEREOTYPE.

is for
LONGITUDINAL STUDIES

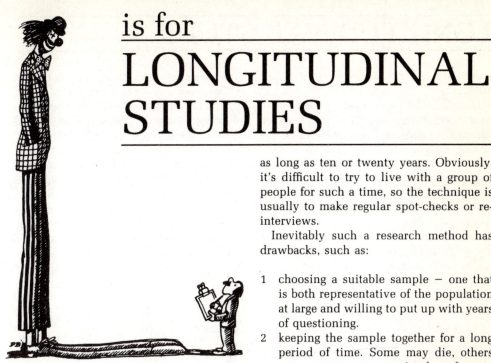

Much social research is like a snapshot. The sociologist interviews or observes the group he is interested in for a day, a week, a month, collates all the information he has collected and comes to some general conclusions. However, such results, though perfectly valid at the time of study, may prove less reliable over the long term. They provide no account of the way in which a particular group develops in its behaviour or views.

Party-political opinion polls are a good example of this. A representative sample interviewed on a Monday may show 60 per cent favouring a new Centre Party, say, but by Friday they may have swung back to Labour. That is why the most accurate polls are those conducted immediately before people vote.

To get round this problem, some sociologists favour what are known as longitudinal studies, which, like a movie film, aim to give a complete picture of the growth and development of the people being studied. The period of study may be as long as ten or twenty years. Obviously, it's difficult to try to live with a group of people for such a time, so the technique is usually to make regular spot-checks or re-interviews.

Inevitably such a research method has drawbacks, such as:

1 choosing a suitable sample – one that is both representative of the population at large and willing to put up with years of questioning.
2 keeping the sample together for a long period of time. Some may die, others may move away or simply refuse to continue the experiment. This raises dangers that the sample will become biased and the results distorted.
3 keeping the same researchers together. Inevitably some of the original investigators are likely to move on to new fields of study and their replacements may alter the direction of the research.
4 keeping the same techniques and classifications. Inevitably existing tests or categories are likely to be found inadequate and replaced by newer ones, but this may make it difficult to compare the later results with earlier ones.
5 cost. The financing of such extended studies is always particularly difficult. Even so, this research technique has proved to be a very rich source of sociological data.

Two particularly fine recent examples have been the study by J.W.B. Douglas of the progress of 5000 babies born in one week in March 1946, and the current National Child Bureau's study of all the ▶

children born in a single week in March 1958.

Douglas' study was based on a simple of over 5000 babies born in one week in March 1946 to represent all children of that age in Britain. Used initially as a study of the effectiveness of ante-natal and maternity services, it proved so valuable that the sample was kept together as a means to studying primary, secondary and further education – and beyond. From this research came Douglas' famous book *Home and School* (1964) which clearly showed not only the influence of home background on educational achievement but the way the school system 'created' success and failure, particularly by streaming pupils.

Its conclusions influenced not only further research but government policy especially in promoting comprehensive education. Through the help of the health and education authorities, costs were kept down and by March 1957 only 4.9% of the children involved had died and 6.7% emigrated. Obviously now the study has extended into further education and work. The 'fall-out' rate is much higher and the dangers of biases greater. Nevertheless studies like these are invaluable. The TV series *Seven Up* and *28 Up* were a fascinating recent example.

See also COMMUNITY.

is for
MARXISM

Karl Marx (1818-83) was one of the founding fathers of sociology. His ideas have always been influential, but since the 1960s they have been the major theoretical influence on the discipline. Basically Marx saw human behaviour as the result of man's social environment. Change society, Marx said, and you change people.

In Marxist theory, society is a totality comprising a superstructure – social institutions such as the family, education and law, all interconnected – based on a substructure, the economy. Marx emphasised the predominant influence of the economic system over all other institutions because it fulfils people's basic needs – food and shelter. And the way people produce their goods determines the way they work and live together.

Marx distinguished, therefore, between the forces of production (the techniques and tools of production) and the relations of production (the social relationships that result from a particular mode of production – for instance, between lord and vassal under feudalism). He saw history as a series of stages, or epochs, developing as people increased their exploitation of nature, from the simple subsistence of earlier times to the abundance of modern industrialism.

Primitive societies tended to produce and share everything in common but as societies advanced so there developed PRIVATE control of the MEANS OF PRODUCTION (the methods, tools and machinery used to produce food and other goods) as one group of individuals or family established its control over the rest and used their power to exploit them. Society become divided into RULING and SUBJECT CLASSES such as the pharaohs and their slaves in Ancient Egypt and the monarchy and the peasantry in feudal times. Such ruling classes ruled not only through force but also through such ideological controls as religion. However, as a new mode of production developed (e.g. as trade and business came to replace agriculture as the main means of production) and as the subject class united and revolted against its exploitation, so a new epoch, a new system of government and economy emerged. Thus in Marx's view of the motor of history, the basis of social change is conflict over control of the means of production – a conflict expressed by the CLASS STRUGGLE.

In his major work *DAS KAPITAL*, Marx made a detailed analysis of the epoch prevailing during his own lifetime – CAPITALISM. Its forces of production – the factory, the mine and the mill – were privately owned. The owners and workers were divided into two main social classes – the BOURGEOISIE and the PROLETARIAT. Though the STATE is still the key organ of class rule (the police, army, etc.), in liberal democracies where people ▸

MARXISM (continued)

have the vote and some apparent control of the government, 'ideological' control is more important than in the past if people are to accept capitalism as fair and natural.

It has to be justified, to appear to be fair, and this is achieved today through the legal and education systems, the welfare state and the mass media. All of these systems appear to work in the interests of all and to be open to all but in fact they primarily serve the interests of the ruling class and help reproduce class relations. The legal and education systems in fact operate in favour of the better-off, the welfare state keeps the workers from starving and so revolting and the media's version of the 'news' is that of the establishment. The workers fail to see the true nature of their exploitation because of FALSE CONSCIOUSNESS and the exclusion of alternative ideas.

Marx argued that like previous epochs, capitalism contains the 'seeds of its own destruction' due to its inherent contradictions. The bourgeoisie needs to maximise profit as one firm competes against another, and so exploits the workers, paying them merely subsistence wages. The difference between what the workers are paid and what the owners take as profit Marx called the surplus value of labour.

In Marx's scenario, the decline of capitalism is heralded by a drop in the number of firms as monopolies are created. The ranks of the proletariat are swelled by bankrupt businessmen, and the workers in the factories become increasingly organised through trade unions, with an increased sense of class-consciousness. Finally, Marx predicted, they would rise up against the bourgeoisie and establish socialism.

He never outlined these final stages in any great detail, but seemed to envisage a social order based initially on a workers' state, 'the Dictatorship of the Proletariat' under which the means of production were communally owned. Since there would then be no conflict of interest or means of exploitation, social classes and even the state would 'wither away'. Wealth would be distributed according to need rather than ability. Work and production would be based on cooperation rather than competition. In a truly COMMUNIST society man's true nature would be liberated and social relationships would be based on harmony rather than conflict and exploitation.

Whilst Marx claimed that his analysis was objective, even scientific and so inevitable, he was also actively involved in promoting revolution in the nineteenth century as he outlined in the Communist Manifesto of 1848. He sought to place the Communist Party as the 'vanguard of the proletariat'. Certainly his ideas have inspired millions of people, especially in poor and exploited countries and have become the basis of many twentieth-century revolutions, though few societies (if any) can truly be called socialist, let alone communist.

Inevitably such a revolutionary doctrine has attracted extensive criticism, in particular:

1 In advanced capitalist societies instead of a polarisation of society into two classes as predicted, a third or MIDDLE CLASS has arisen and grown, acting as a buffer between the bourgeoisie and proletariat and allowing social mobility.

2 Similarly, instead of the working classes in advanced capitalist societies becoming increasingly united and class-conscious, moving from being a 'class in itself' to a 'class for itself' they remain essentially conservative and non-revolutionary. Even with today's three million unemployed and capitalism in Britain in great financial crisis, a radical Tory government was returned to power in 1983 via the votes of skilled and even unemployed workers. In fact no advanced capitalist society has gone communist. Only agrarian ones like

Russia and China have – and they more by political force than by economic change.

3 So-called communist societies, though they have significantly raised the standard of living of their people, have also developed inequalities almost as great as those in capitalist societies and the individual is certainly less free. The Dictatorship of the Proletariat has often turned out to be the dictatorship of the Communist Party.

4 Marx's analysis of history and society put prime emphasis on ECONOMIC factors. Others have accused him of 'economic determinism' and argued that other factors are equally important – e.g. Max Weber claimed that the Protestant Ethic was also crucial in 'sparking off' industrial revolutions in the West. In fact Marx's analysis allowed for a lot more interaction between economic, political and cultural factors than he is often given credit for.

5 At times he seems to portray human beings as puppets of economic forces, unable to control their own destiny. In fact the whole of Marx's analysis was one of hope. He hoped to show the mass of the people how to liberate themselves from the apparently inexorable forces of the market by showing them that behind such forces were people, the bourgeoisie. As he proclaimed, 'man makes his own history', and so he encouraged the workers to throw off their chains and fight for control of their lives by force if necessary – by the ballot box if possible.

Many of the criticisms of Marxism are more those of his followers than of Marx himself. He has had a profound influence on modern thinking and a great deal of both early and modern sociology has been a debate with 'the ghost of Marx' (e.g. the writings of Max Weber). Modern or neo-Marxism has involved attempts to apply Marx's ideas to areas he only touched on (e.g. organisations, gender, urban sociology) or to re-analyse areas that have since changed. For example:

(i) CLASS – the growth and heterogeneity of the modern middle class, new forms of property ownership and shareholding and the lack of proletarian radicalism have all necessitated rethinking (see CLASS, MIDDLE CLASS and PROLETARIAT).

(ii) POLITICS – the modern democratic state is not obviously controlled by the bourgeoisie (as in the nineteenth century) but by the people via elections. Modern Marxists seek to prove that such democracy is a sham and that the ruling class is really in control (see ELITE and POWER) but disagree over whether such control is by members of the bourgeoisie actually running the government, civil service, police, army and legal system or whether the modern state is 'relatively autonomous', acting in the long-term interests of capital, yet having sufficient independence to, when necessary, grant concessions to buy off the workers (e.g. the welfare state) or force 'fractions' of the capitalist class to unite despite occasional conflicts of interest between them (e.g. between, say, financiers and businessmen over the rate of interest). This is often referred to as the Miliband-Poulantzas Debate.

(iii) IDEOLOGY – with ideological control so crucial in advanced democratic society, A. Gramsci and Louis Althusser proposed the concept of HEGEMONY, that through the education system and media the ruling class has persuaded the mass of people to accept their ideas, views and values as normal and natural. Alternatives are never seriously considered. This concept is a modern version of Marx's idea of false consciousness and is used to explain the modern working classes' lack of revolutionary ardour. Bowles and Gintis (*Schooling in Capitalist America*, 1976), for example, see the education ▶

MARXISM (continued)

system not as open and meritocratic but merely having this appearance. In fact the 'well-off' do well and the working classes fail but because the system seems fair, the dominance of the bourgeoisie seems legitimate because they seem to be the ablest in society (see also PROFESSIONS).

(iv) THE ROLE OF WOMEN – has been extensively re-analysed by feminists, many using a Marxist perspective (see GENDER).

(v) OTHER EXAMPLES includes URBAN SOCIOLOGY (p. 116) and DEVELOPMENT.

Certainly in the 1970s and 1980s, amid economic and social depression Marxism has enjoyed a substantial revival and has a particularly powerful influence on modern sociology.

See also FUNCTIONALISM, INTERACTIONISM, CAPITALISM.

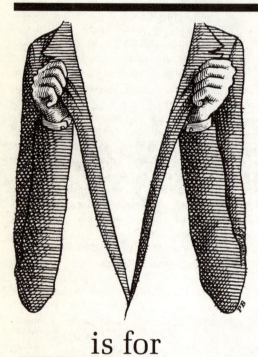

is for
MERITOCRACY

society, with the education system as the chief means of promoting and selecting talent. Thus, according to the theory, the best people are fitted to the best jobs.

'Meritocrats' believe that the school system should be as open as possible to increase motivation and competition and ensure equal opportunity for all. This way it is hoped that social mobility, especially for the lower classes, will be increased, and privilege and favouritism eliminated. The comprehensive schools were set up in the 1960s and 1970s with these principles in mind.

Functionalist writers, too, support the idea of meritocracy. According to their analysis of society (see FUNCTIONALISM, p. 40), it is vital that the ablest people take on the most difficult and responsible tasks. In a famous article in 1945 ('Some Principles of Stratification') Davies and Moore argued that the key mechanism 'by which

The *Oxford Dictionary* defines merit as worth or excellence and meritocracy as a 'system of government or control by persons of practical or intellectual ability'. Many liberal reformers in the west believe that merit is the ideal way to organise

societies insure that the most important positions are conscientiously filled by the most qualified people' is the system of social stratification evident in all known human societies. The high rewards and special status attached to society's 'top jobs' are the means by which the ablest in society are motivated to compete for such positions, are willing to put up with the sacrifices involved in long periods of training and gaining qualifications and are prepared to work hard and endure the stress involved. Only by attracting the ablest to the key roles can society be sure of efficient functioning; failure to do so threatens its very survival. Such writers assume, however, that the existing system of social mobility and role allocation, as say, modern America, is truly meritocratic – open to all, fair and based solely on ability. Critics like Melvin Tumin have severely questioned such an assumption, arguing that the functionalist model of social mobility completely ignores the crucial influence of power and class background on people's opportunities in life. Numerous studies have shown that boys, whites, and the middle classes have far more chance of reaching the top than do girls, blacks and the working classes.

Marxist writers go even further. In their view the whole idea of meritocracy is a phoney one used to justify and camouflage the underlying inequalities and conflicts of a class society. For example, by appearing to be open the education system claims that those who do best at school are the most able, and so deserve the top jobs. The Marxists believe that educational and occupational achievements are more likely to be related to family background. The children of the wealthy and powerful, they say, tend to obtain high qualifications and top jobs irrespective of ability. For writers like Samuel Bowles and Herbert Gintis (*Schooling in Capitalist Society*, 1976) the education system is a giant myth-making machine, legitimising inequality because 'its apparent social mobility takes the steam out of working-class discontent and hides the injustice of privilege breeding privilege'. Education can only reflect the social system, not change it.

The British sociologist Michael Young makes different, but no less sweeping criticisms. In his satire, *The Rise of the Meritocracy* (1958), he imagined a future British society in which the most able people filled the most important positions in society. With everyone having equal opportunity to realise their talents and skills, selection and social status were based solely on merit.

This, however, left the lower classes totally demoralised. There was no longer any excuse for their lowly position. In a society where everyone is encouraged to try to reach the top, failure can be especially hard to bear, and with no people of ability in their ranks they lacked effective leadership and representation. Similarly the upper classes were now certain of their superiority. No longer inhibited by fears of possible opposition or competition from the lower classes, they ruled society with arrogance and cynicism.

See also SOCIAL MOBILITY.

PB

is for

MIDDLE CLASS

professional classes, who respectively comprise about 14 per cent and 12 per cent of the total work-force in Britain. The higher professional classes comprise such occupations as judges, barristers, and engineers. The lower professionals tend to be teachers, nurses, social workers and so on.

The classification, 'middle class' also includes owners of small businesses – a declining group (about 2–4 per cent of the total working population) – and managers and administrators who, in contrast, have grown from about 5.5 per cent of workers in 1951 to nearly 9 per cent today. However, being middle-class is more than just a job, it's a way of life distinguished by a particular lifestyle and set of values – affluence, conservatism (with both a big and a small c) and respectability. Middle-class people usually enjoy higher-than-

A major characteristic of modern industrial societies has been the growth and predominance of a middle class. This comes between the tiny upper class of wealthy property-owners, and the mass of the population – usually called the working class. It is defined by the Registrar General (and by most sociologists) in terms of occupations – non-manual occupations that require brains rather than brawn. The middle class is usually further divided into higher and lower professional, managerial and administrative, and those in clerical and minor supervisory positions. These are classes I, II and III on the Registrar General's scale.

This white-collar sector, as it is often called, has expanded considerably with the growth of bureaucracy in modern industry, government and the welfare state. The two key areas of expansion here are the clerical sector (though much of this reflects the increased employment of women) and the

average incomes and secure jobs, with opportunities for 'perks' and promotion. They usually own their own homes, have small families, and do well out of our education and health systems. Such an occupational and social background inevitably influences middle-class people's view of the social structure and their position in it – their self-assigned class. While few managers or professionals doubt their middle-classness, surveys in the 1950s showed that around 25 per cent of clerks saw themselves as working-class, and between 30 per cent and 50 per cent voted Labour. (Such studies often hinge on the respondents' interpretation of the term 'working-class'. Some may feel that anybody who works for a living is working-class.)

Various studies have shown that while working-class people tend to hold collectivist attitudes and a power-model view of society as 'us and them' the middle class are more individualistic, seeing society as a sort of ladder up which anybody with ability and ambition can climb.

Recent studies show that the modern middle class is best conceived of as a series of 'middle classes'. Rather than one homogeneous bloc such intermediate groups are growing in size and in variety. The Oxford Mobility Study showed the middle classes to be very heterogeneous whilst Ken Roberts *et al*'s study of Liverpool showed four different middle-class 'fragments' (*The Fragmentary Class Structure*, 1977):

1   Those who saw themselves as part of a 'middle mass' made up of the bulk of the working population sandwiched between a small, rich and powerful upper class and a relatively impoverished lower class (27% of sample)
2   Those who saw themselves as part of a 'compressed middle class' squeezed between a powerful upper class and the working class, with the government, big business and the unions as their enemies; a 'typical small businessman's view' (19½% of sample)
3   Those who saw society as a ladder open to all. They generally rejected the idea of a class society. This view was mainly held by the well-educated in professional occupations with high incomes (15%)
4   Those with a proletarian view of society

and claiming to be working-class. They were usually in routine white-collar occupations with low wages and few promotion prospects.

Thus, though the trend in advanced industrial societies has been towards an expansion of the middle classes, this does not necessarily prove the EMBOURGEOISEMENT THESIS correct (see p. 30). Yet such intermediate groups have been of central concern to modern stratification analyses. Marxist writers in particular have had to grapple with fitting the growth of the middle classes into their overall theory that advanced capitalist societies should polarise into two major classes.

One attempt has been the PROLETARIANISATION THESIS (see p. 85) that the lower middle-class group are in fact part of the proletariat in terms of income, conditions, unionism and supervision. Others see the new middle class as in a contradictory position enjoying certain of the privileges of the bourgeoisie and having some control over others and over themselves yet ultimately they too are exploited (E.O. Wright). Such writers distinguish between the top and lower levels of the middle class and between the professional and managerial groups according to their 'life-chances' and market position. Anthony Giddens (*The Class Structure of Advanced Societies*, 1973) identifies three main classes – the Upper, Intermediate and Working Class.

See also CLASS, EMBOURGEOISEMENT, PROFESSIONS.

is for
NORMS

In the simplest terms, norms are the shared values that people have as to what is regarded as correct and acceptable behaviour in society. These obviously vary between societies, cultures, ages and groups – even between one situation and another.

Norms extend right from central guidelines like those concerning incest, cannibalism and murder to such apparently trivial customs as the right colour to wear at a funeral or the correct way to hold a knife and fork. These norms of behaviour are learnt through socialisation. As children grow up, they quickly learn what is considered appropriate behaviour. By adulthood they have internalised these guidelines almost as a form of conscience, an inner sense of what is right or what ought to be done in a given situation. Such socialisation is reinforced by various rewards and sanctions, some informal – such as a disapproving glance or a word of praise – others formal, such as imprisonment or promotion.

Thus norms are a key element in social control (see p. 100). Though it is relatively easy to explain the origins of laws against, say, murder or robbery, it is not so easy to explain the basis of norms governing, say, the entry of a woman into a pub on her own, since these depend more on specific situations.

Often we know that a certain type of behaviour is wrong, but we're not sure why, especially when it has gained the sanctity of religious custom or tradition. Most of us know, for example, that the eating of pork is forbidden to Jews and Mohammedans, but not everyone knows the origins of this norm. It may be due to the fact that in the countries where these two religions arose, meat is likely to go bad very quickly because of the heat.

The concept of norms of social behaviour gained particular prominence in sociology through functionalist views of society, particularly those of Talcott Parsons. Like Emile Durkheim, Parsons believed that only a commitment to common values would provide a basis for social order, a 'system' of regulatory, normative rules, otherwise chaos would result. For society to function properly, such rules must not only be enforced by external sanctions but also be internalised and seen as morally correct.

While other sociologists have disagreed with so organised and orderly a view of social life, few discount the importance of social norms as a key influence on individual and group behaviour.

See also CULTURE, SUB-CULTURE, SOCIALISATION.

is for
OBJECTIVITY

The ability to make an impartial and balanced assessment of a situation or given set of facts without favour or bias, and without allowing personal opinions to colour the final conclusions, is considered crucial to all forms of academic study if truth and knowledge are to be discovered. It is considered especially vital to scientific research because scientists see the natural world as governed by laws of cause and effect, which can only come to light through logical analysis and rigorous experimentation. Subjective factors and value judgements as to whether a particular form of research into, say, nuclear power is good or bad are considered irrelevant, even distorting. Rather, it is said, 'the facts should be allowed to speak for themselves'.

However, it is much more difficult for social scientists to be objective:

1   They haven't got the controlled conditions of a laboratory to work in but are usually dealing with complex social situations, sometimes from the past, that cannot be repeated or easily broken down into key variables

2   Unlike natural phenomena, their subjects are complex, unstable human beings with a will of their own and for whom emotion is a key influence on behaviour

3   Most especially, being human themselves, social scientists find it very difficult totally to divorce personal attitudes, values and prejudices from their professional analysis of other humans.

Their presence may influence the behaviour or answers of the people they are studying. Yet they must be objective if their researches in particular and sociology in general are even to gain the status of being considered scientific. Max Weber was particularly concerned that sociology be value-free and not dismissed as merely common sense or, worse, polemic and ideology. However, some of the newer trends in sociology not only reject the idea of it becoming a science, but consider objectivity both an impossible goal and the wrong way for sociologists to gain real insight into human behaviour.

They see the natural and social worlds as fundamentally different. Whilst 'facts' about the natural world may be objective (and some scientists today question this), may have an existence independent of outside observers, social facts do not. Rather they are created by people's social interactions and only exist through the meanings people give to a particular situation or form of behaviour. All social knowledge is thus RELATIVE, it depends on how people see it; it cannot exist on its own. For example, whilst such natural phenomena as trees and mountains continue to exist whether people are there to observe them or not, such social phenomena as crime do not. Crimes are merely forms of behaviour that people (in authority) have so labelled but it ▶

also depends on the situation involved. There is for example a thin line between rape and making love, between boxing and GBH.

It all depends on interpretation. A man alone in a room on his knees may be praying or going mad, depending on how that form of behaviour in that situation is interpreted. Thus, for phenomenologists, the key to social knowledge is not impartial observation and logical analysis but the understanding of a situation from the participant's point of view. Rather than withdraw his emotional and human faculties, the sociologist should use empathy, even intuition, to increase his understanding of social 'reality'. Otherwise the sociologist will impose his own logical analysis on a situation he only partially understands — especially if the basis of his knowledge is survey or statistical material which conveys little real 'meaning'.

Phenomenologists argue that value-freedom (objectivity) is an illusion. No sociologist can escape from the influence of his own past experiences, his cultural background and taken-for-granted assumptions. No facts have meaning outside a given set of underlying assumptions and concepts by which the researcher makes sense of them. If carefully analysed such assumptions constitute an IDEOLOGY (see p. 50), a particular framework or view of the world into which such facts are fitted and made sense of.

Marxist writers put this even more strongly and believe that such personal frameworks are conditioned by the dominant ideology of a particular period of history, be it feudalism or capitalism. By such ideologies the ruling class of such epochs controls people's ideas and gains support and legitimisation for their power.

Marxists believe that even so-called 'objective' analysis has an ideological basis and if it fails to criticise the existing social order, it is by implication supporting it and may thus be labelled conservative, even reactionary. For Marxists social knowledge can never be neutral and they would wish sociology to adopt a value-laden critical stance in its analysis. In a sense they too are claiming 'objectivity' to the extent that they claim that theirs is a clearer, more scientific analysis of social power, justice and reality.

Thus modern sociology is no longer united under one pathway to truth and objectivity as it seemed to be under Functionalism in the 1950s but is faced by a number of perspectives each with an 'ideological' bias, be it to conservatism (functionalism) or radicalism (Marxism). However, most sociologists, whilst recognising the validity of much of the above, still feel that objectivity in the scientific and judicial sense is still an ideal worth pursuing if the discipline is not to disappear into pure relativism and polemic. Many, like Anthony Giddens, follow Weber in seeking to combine 'interpretation' with value-freedom in their analyses.

See also IDEOLOGY, POSITIVISM, SUBJECTIVITY.

is for

PARTICIPANT OBSERVATION

when I do something I have to think what Bill Whyte would want to know about it. Before, I used to do things by instinct.'

The initial problem such researchers face is that of 'getting into' the group involved. Some managed this through previous contact with a member of the group, as Howard Parker did in his study of the 'Roundhouse' boys in Liverpool. Festinger *et al.* used fake stories to gain entry to a religious cult. A great deal depends on the sociologist's own personality and style. As Parker comments, 'If I hadn't been young, hairy, boozy, etc., the liaison would have

Simple observation of, say, a group of teenagers or strikers will tell sociologists what they are doing, but only by participating in people's activities will a real understanding be gained of why they are behaving as they are. Such participation can be fairly limited as, for example, in mingling with a football crowd. On the other hand, the observer might actually join the group under study – a religious cult, for instance.

Obviously such involvement raises the danger that researchers will become so immersed in the group's activities and values that their analysis will become biased and unobjective. Their presence may influence the group's activities to the extent that its members no longer behave 'naturally' – and become observers themselves.

The American soiologist W.F. Whyte, who made a famous study of a Chicago street-corner gang in the 1930s, found that the gang's leader, Doc, became a 'true collaborator in research'. This greatly helped Whyte's understanding, but led Doc to remark: 'You've slowed me up plenty. Now

failed'.

Once in, the researcher has to get into a position that will maximise his knowledge. Tom Lupton's jobs as a 'smearer' and a 'sweeper' in a factory allowed him to circulate freely; Roland Frankenberg actually became secretary of the football club of the village he was observing. But how involved should a sociologist become? Ned Polsky has argued for complete immersion even to the point of joining in a robbery, Howard Parker was prepared to receive 'knock-off', and in observing a Glasgow gang James Patrick was abused by others for not joining in a gang-fight but gained minimum acceptance by being picked up by the police.

Finally there is the problem of knowing what to observe and how to record it. Asking questions generally leads to suspicion and cautious responses. Most sociologists in this field prefer to become part of the scenery, so accepted that no one notices them and so everyone talks freely. By such a technique the researcher also learns the MEANING behind what is being said and done, the group's own rituals, ▶

PARTICIPANT OBSERVATION (continued)

slang and even sub-culture. Making notes – so vital to this methodology – is not always easy and can be precarious if the researcher has not revealed his true identity. Festinger et al. had to go to the bathroom very regularly and use midget tape recorders.

Participant observation is difficult, time-consuming, and by its apparent concentration on deviant groups, occasionally dangerous. But its advantages, if well done, are enormous in terms of understanding social reality without sociologists imposing their own interpretation and values on events. It claims to achieve a high degree of VALIDITY.

For this reason, it is very popular with those who favour the phenomenological perspective in sociology. It is, however, criticised as unreliable by positivists (sociologists who believe sociology should try to emulate the techniques of the natural sciences, and so are particularly concerned about the researcher's objectivity and impartiality).

The conclusions and generalisations generated by such studies are not necessarily applicable to any other situation, the positivists say, and so have only limited value in developing sociological theories. Further, they cannot be replicated and checked by other researchers since so much depends on the researchers themselves – their personality, sensitivity and interpretative skills. The classic example of this problem was Oscar Lewis's re-study of the Mexican village Tepoztlan (*Life in a Mexican Village*, 1951); where a previous researcher, Robert Redfield, had found harmony and love, Lewis found conflict and tension. They were using different perspectives and so came up with different answers.

Participant observation is an intensely personal, even subjective form of study, involving on-the-spot judgements about such minutiae as tones of voice, gestures and modes of dress. As W.F. Whyte comments, 'I began as a non-participating observer. As I became accepted into the community I found myself becoming almost a non-observing participant'. Yet it is objective in the sense that it seeks to understand social reality from the point of view of those involved rather than simply that of the researcher.

See also INTERACTIONISM, PHENOMENOLOGY.

Such groups develop their own set of NORMS (see p. 68), supported by a system of rewards and sanctions to ensure conformity and punish deviance. Even amongst young school children there is a certain withdrawal from the world of adults (parents and teachers) within which certain standards of behaviour are expected such as the keeping of secrets and not 'snitching' on each other. To go against such norms is to risk such punishments as being 'sent to Coventry' or being terrorised. Such groups even develop STATUS hierarchies by which the most intelligent, popular or aggressive achieve predominant status, even group leadership.

However, whilst the playground world of young school children has rarely been referred to as a SUB-CULTURE (see p. 112) the more intimate, isolated and withdrawn

is for
PEER GROUPS

This term can be most simply defined as a group of people with similar status, interests and/or age or race or any other common characteristic with whom an individual identifies. More specifically it refers to people of equal rank, merit or quality and so a peer group represents a group of equals. Hence the term 'peers of the realm' to refer to members of the House of Lords. However within sociology this term is mainly associated with children and adolescent groups who associate together. Such groups are a crucial part of the socialisation process because for the first time the child is learning how to get on with others of a similar age in a group situation. Previously the key influences on its behaviour have been older people, particularly its parents. Now at playgroup or infant school it is having to learn how to integrate into informal social groups where the rules and norms are not formally explained nor gently taught and it learns how to treat the opposite sex.

world of adolescents has. A whole range of studies about such 'youth culture' have been produced in the post-war period seeking to analyse the extent to which the lifestyles of juvenile gangs — mods, rockers, punks, hippies — seriously constitute a sub-culture. A classic example of such a study was Paul Willis's book *Learning to Labour* (1978) in which he sought to show in detail not only the lifestyle of working-class adolescents but how 'working-class kids get working-class jobs'.

Rejecting the middle-class world of school and its status system of academic success, such 'lads' establish an alternative, anti-school culture in which having a laugh, fighting and avoiding or defying school discipline are key elements. Thus though they escape the conformity of the school system, they are unwittingly preparing themselves for the harsh discipline and routine of unskilled factory work. Peter Wilmott's earlier study *Adolescent Boys in East London* (1966) similarly found the ▶

main characteristics of working-class adolescent peer groups to be a desire for fun or 'kicks', a rejection of authority, a strong sense of territory and a predominantly masculine emphasis on physical strength, skill and daring, whether on a motorcycle or in a fight. Music and clothes are important background features of such sub-cultures.

Such features have been seized upon by the media and consumer industries as the means to marketing a whole new range of goods and services. Whilst many sociologists of the 1960s referred to such adolescent ways of life as distinct sub-cultures, more recent work questions this, arguing that such characteristics are exaggerated forms of 'class' behaviour (as in the dress of, say, 'skinheads') and that most adolescents merely go through a phase of breaking away from adult authority, of expressing their independence through clothes and music before settling down. Much of their distinctiveness is exaggerated, particularly by the media and advertising. Their basic values are in fact very similar to those of adults.

This discussion is part of the Functionalist-Marxist debate on Youth Culture. (See SUB-CULTURE p. 112.)

The term 'peer group' can usefully be applied to any age or status group, particularly in work situations. For example, the well-known Hawthorne Studies of the 1920s and 1930s revealed the way informal workgroups are often the key factor determining worker-productivity. This study of men wiring up telephone equipment showed that the men did not work as individuals, all aiming to produce the most and so earn the maximum bonuses, but conformed to an informal group norm producing sufficient units to keep the supervisor happy but not enough to give the management an excuse to lower the basic rate, or cut the workforce. Those who failed to conform to this informal 'work rate' were labelled 'speedkings' or chislers and the others ganged up on them. In strike situations the term 'blackleg' is used similarly.

Thus peer groups are not only important forms of SOCIALISATION but also of SOCIAL CONTROL (see pp. 102, 107).

See also GROUPS, SOCIALISATION, STATUS.

is for

PHENOMENO-LOGY

logists say, is not a thing out there with a life of its own controlling us, but something we create every day through our normal activities and routines, and through the common assumptions we use to deal with others. A key element in constructing social reality and in communicating our interpretations to others is LANGUAGE.

But, you may ask, if everybody is operating according to their own personal view of the world, why isn't there total anarchy? One writer, Alfred Schultz, argues that order is achieved first through our taken-for-granted assumptions – our expectations of what should happen in a normal day and how we expect others to act. We expect the milk and papers to arrive, we expect everyone else in the office to be working. Second, this social fabric is maintained by what Schultz called typifications – common ways of classifying objects (house, man) and experiences (nightmare, hate) but ways which are capable of redefinition and adaptation. Thus a man dressed as a priest will get a different reaction from one dressed as a policeman. Thirdly, order is maintained by RECIPROCITY, by our acting on the assumption that others see the world in the same way as we do – obviously this does not always work: we have all had experiences of being misunderstood, of talking at cross-purposes.

Phenomenology is the basis of several of the newer approaches in sociology, particularly of symbolic interactionism. It poses a radical challenge to the scientific basis of most traditional areas of the subject. The word PHENOMENON may be defined as either 'a fact or occurence' or as 'an object of perception'. The first definition is the scientific one and believes that things in the external world really do exist; the second definition refers to the way our brain interprets what our senses perceive and so makes sense of reality. This is the basis of phenomenology.

For phenomenologists, our social world is relative. We give everything a label and so a meaning. For example, we call certain wooden objects chairs and others tables and we use them for different purposes. But while such physical objects have an existence of their own, social facts do not. Thus whilst a physical object such as a forest will continue to exist whether or not there are people around to define it, the existence of such social 'facts' as war or unemployment depends on common agreement between two or more people.

Similarly, such social facts change as the situation does. For example killing someone is defined as murder in peacetime, heroism in wartime. Society, phenomeno-

All three elements of this inter-subjectivity are not only learnt through socialisation, but are also 'mental tools' which we carry around with us so that we can adapt our behaviour according to the situation we find ourselves in.

Two people alone in a room might indicate a lesson, an interview, a confession. How do we decide which?

Thus phenomenology has challenged ▶

'scientific' sociology on two main levels: (a) its view of man and society; (b) its method of research.

1 Whilst 'scientific' sociology tends to REIFY society, to portray it as something above and beyond the individual, as something with a reality, a life of its own, phenomenologists see it as something we humans create and re-create in our everyday interactions and routines – it's all in our minds. Similarly whilst social scientists tend to portray people as puppets, their behaviour largely determined by such external forces as the economy and the environment, phenomenology sees people as free and independent agents capable of constructing and controlling their own environment or world, with the power to determine their own future. We don't have to be chained to our social roles and responsibilities – we have the power to break free if we choose. Man's actions are therefore not simply reactions to external influences, not instinctive but purposeful and motivated.

2 Thus in the view of phenomenologists our social world is fundamentally different to the natural one and so the scientific methods of natural scientists are totally inappropriate because they fail to take the subject's own view into account and assume the possibility of OBJECTIVITY. In the phenomenologist's view a social situation can only be truly understood from the actor's own point of view and so the sociologist should not be detached but try through his own humanness – his empathy and intui-

tion, to see the world in the same way that the people he is studying do. Only then can he understand their feelings and motives. Hence the phenomenologist's preference for such interpretative techniques as PARTICIPANT OBSERVATION (see p. 71). Similarly they see objectivity as impossible because facts cannot speak for themselves, and inevitably this involves the sociologist using his own values and taken-for-granted assumptions in interpreting them.

Thus in their view a great deal of so-called scientific research reflects not the views and attitudes of ordinary people, but those of the sociologists doing the research. Similarly, they reject such social facts as statistics on crime and suicide as being representative of criminal behaviour. Rather, such facts are in a sense created by those collecting, classifying and interpreting them and by others involved in this social process. Thus for example a rise in the crime rate may not represent more crime being committed but simply more policemen being employed or more laws being made. Phenomenology has set sociology off in important new directions and provides valuable insights into the behaviour of small-scale groups. But its relativism borders on psychology, and it lacks the breadth and thus the attractiveness of the grander theories which claim to be able to explain major social problems, and even predict the future. Nevertheless, its impact on modern sociology has been both dramatic and stimulating.

See also POSITIVISM, INTERACTIONISM.

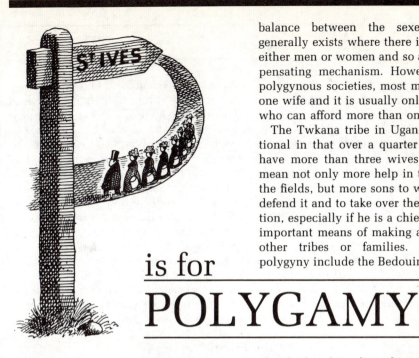

is for

POLYGAMY

balance between the sexes, polygamy generally exists where there is a surplus of either men or women and so acts as a compensating mechanism. However, even in polygynous societies, most men have only one wife and it is usually only the wealthy who can afford more than one dowry.

The Twkana tribe in Uganda are exceptional in that over a quarter of their men have more than three wives. Extra wives mean not only more help in the home and the fields, but more sons to work the land, defend it and to take over the father's position, especially if he is a chief. It is also an important means of making alliances with other tribes or families. Examples of polygyny include the Bedouin of Niger and the sheiks of Saudi Arabia.

Polygamy is a term we use to describe a marriage where one person has two or more partners. When a man is allowed to marry more than one woman it is called polygyny. Polyandry means that a woman may take more than one husband. In Britain we practise monogamy, whereby a person can legally only have one husband or wife at a time. We have strict social conventions to protect this relationship, particularly against adultery. In fact bigamy — marriage to more than one partner — is an offence against the law and the whole idea of multiple marriage seems strange to us — even rather wicked.

However, anthropological research has shown that in those societies that still practise it, far from being immoral, polygamy fulfils vital social and economic needs. It functions as an outlet for the sex-drive, and as a means of producing and caring for children and giving them a legitimate place in society, an organised means of passing on wealth and a way of ensuring a sufficient labour force.

In contrast to monogamy, which is usually practised in societies with a

Polyandry is much more unusual, and generally involves brothers sharing the same wife. This happens among some people in Tibet, where conditions are harsh and resources scarce. Such a relationship means that the division of property becomes unnecessary. The young men of the Leletribe in central Africa also practise polyandry, but this is because the older men have the right to more than one wife and there are not enough marriageable girls left for the rest of the tribe.

Polygamy is thus a vital part of such societies' social structures. No society could easily withstand the pressures of large numbers of unmarried men or women and, inevitably, large numbers of uncared-for children. Such relationships are usually conducted aaccording to a strict set of rules and in polygynous households there is normally a hierarchy of senior and junior wives and a strict rota of duties.

But why do such surpluses occur in the first place? Among the contributory factors is the general trend that though more boys are born than girls, more die in the first ▶

POLYGAMY (continued)

year or so. More men usually die in war-time than women, and often women live longer than men. Westernisation, however, has considerably affected such traditions. Modern health and hygiene have altered the balance of the sexes, missionaries and commercialism have encouraged the abolition of what are seen as primitive practices, and industrialisation has turned farmers into wage-earners for whom extra wives are now an economic liability rather than an asset.

Obviously a key element in all marriage systems is religion and whilst Christianity has provided the ethical foundation for western monogamy the Koran has been interpreted so as to allow men up to four wives, plus concubines. In Islamic societies not only is divorce very easy for men (but difficult for women) but under their laws of inheritance men benefit twice as much as women. The Hindu religion also regards women as inferior to men and best suited to producing children. Hence the practices of child-marriages to ensure maximum production of children and of SUTTEE, when the wife throws herself on her husband's funeral pyre. Suttee is now both illegal and relatively rare.

Thus though wickedly attractive to us in the West, polygamy does fulfil social as well as sexual functions and continues to exist even in societies facing rapid social change such as Saudi Arabia today.

See also KINSHIP

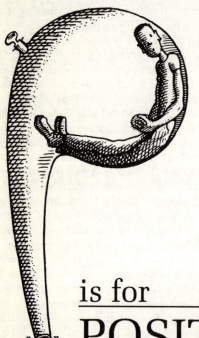

is for
POSITIVISM

Positivism is the term used to describe the approach of those sociologists who believe that the most accurate method of studying human social behaviour is through the techniques developed by the natural sciences. Positivists set out to discover what August Comte called 'the invariable laws governing the evolution of society'. According to Graham Sergeant (*A Textbook of Sociology*, second edition 1979), a science can be defined as either:

1 a body of organised, verified knowledge developed through systematic investigation or
2 a method by which such knowledge is accumulated.

Not having achieved the first definition in the way the natural sciences have, sociology has attempted to develop a similar methodology.

The key characteristics of SCIENTIFIC METHOD can be listed as:

Intersubjective reliability − the ability of information to be re-tested and so verified or altered by independent observers

Objectivity − the ability of the researcher to be totally impartial

Quantifiability − the ability of the subject-matter involved to be precisely measured, so that controlled experiments to test the causal relationships of two or more variables can be conducted, and predictions about future behaviour made. For example, fixed quantities of chemicals A and B always produce an explosion of X power.

Positivism works on one fundamental assumption − that behaviour in the natural and social worlds is governed by the same principles. Just as the behaviour of atoms and molecules is determined primarily by external stimuli so, too, the positivists say, is that of human beings. Human behaviour can be measured, and cause-and-effect relationships developed to the point where it will be possible to construct laws and even predictions about human behaviour. The positivist perspective considers motives or feelings irrelevant since they cannot be observed nor measured.

This faith in the scientific method dates back to the founding fathers of sociology and their desire to raise the subject to the status of the natural sciences. A classic example of this approach was Durkheim's study of suicide, in which he sought to show that suicide is not simply an individual act, but a product of social forces. Modern social science has adopted the sophisticated techniques of mathematical and computer sciences as represented in modern survey analysis, psephology (see p. 87) and the work of the American sociologist Harvey Brenner, trying to correlate the social effects (rise in crime, divorce, suicides, etc.) of a percentage rise in unemployment.

However, positivism has been attacked on the ground that:

1 Sociology can never become a science in the truest sense of the word.
2 It is wrong for sociology even to try to do so.

The first criticism rests on the idea that in studying human behaviour, sociology can do little more than become a second-rate science.

(a) Its researches are rarely reliable or verifiable by other sociologists, since it is very difficult precisely to repeat a survey or interview, since so much depends on the skill of the original researcher.
(b) It is very difficult to be truly objective in conducting social research. The researcher's presence, questions and dress may all influence people's answers. His attitudes and personal views are bound to have some influence on the way he writes up his researches.
(c) It is impossible to measure and quantify human behaviour in the same way as that of rocks or rats. Sociologists rarely have controlled conditions to work in such as the scientist's laboratory.

Sociologists have thus so far failed to produce any theories or laws of nature comparable in standing and power of prediction to those of Newton, Einstein or Darwin − though Durkheim, Weber and especially Marx have profoundly influenced human ideas. The second criticism of positivism is more fundamental.

1 Phenomenologists reject the positivist assumption that natural and social phenomena are essentially the same, and are subject to the same laws of behaviour. For phenomenologists, man does not simply react to external forces like a puppet on a string, but is an active conscious being with a will of his own.
2 Both phenomenologists and Marxists challenge the concept of objectivity in ▶

social research, but in different ways. Phenomenologists say it is impossible for people to discard their own taken-for-granted assumptions about the world. Marxists in contrast argue that all existing knowledge is ideological in the sense that it is a reflection of the ideas and values of the ruling class of a particular epoch. Only Marxism, they argue, offers a truly objective view of the reality of capitalist society and only in a classless society will false consciousness be eliminated.

Nevertheless the attraction of scientific status is still very powerful and even Marxists claim a scientific basis for their theories of social development.

See also PHENOMENOLOGY, OBJECTIVITY.

is for POWER

Power is one of the most elusive of sociological concepts because of the huge variety of forms it comes in and the difficulties of identifying and measuring it. The American political scientist Robert A. Dahl defined power as 'the ability of A to get B to do what B would not otherwise have done', while Max Weber saw it as 'the chance of a man or a number of men to realise their own will in a communal action even against the resistance of others who are participating in the action'. Essentially it is the ability of an individual or group to get what they want, but no one holds power in isolation; it is always power in relation to or over others.

The range of types of power is enormous, stretching from 'persuasion' and 'influence' through to 'force' and 'coercion'. It is similarly important to distinguish between FORMAL and INFORMAL POWER, between power(s) that go with a particular office or job such as that of Prime Minister or Headmaster and those more personal powers particular individuals have or acquire over others by virtue of their personality or relationship with others. Often the two may be combined, as in the dominant personality of Mrs Thatcher within the office of Prime Minister. A major type of formal power is AUTHORITY, power generally accepted as legitimate or lawful and so readily obeyed.

Max Weber, for example, distinguished between three main types of authority:

CHARISMA — authority based on people's devotion and loyalty to a particular leader because of his/her exceptional qualities, abilities and most of all their personal magnetism (e.g. Jesus)

TRADITION — authority based on past customs, on the traditional structure of power as, say, in people's devotion to monarchy

RATIONAL/LEGAL — authority based on formal, impersonal and rational rules and positions of power established by a publically accepted system of law-making. Thus we obey the traffic laws and accept the authority of a policeman or judge, irrespective of the individual involved, because we accept the legitimacy of the system of government that created them. Such rules have a rational or logical purpose and are designed to achieve a specific goal and to limit the power of the person enforcing them.

Whilst in Weber's view authority in past societies was based primarily on charisma and tradition, the key feature of advanced industrial societies is the move to a system of government and social organisation based on rules and rational action (see BUREAUCRACY, p. 6).

A distinction can also be made between ACTUAL power — the actual exercise of power as, say, in punishing someone — and POTENTIAL power, a sort of reservoir of power as, say when a pupil does not leave the classroom, because he knows the teacher would stop him if he tried. Often such distinctions overlap, as happens when the government reinforces its authority by using coercion or force in the form of the police or army.

The sources of power are similarly endless — economic, political, social, cultural, ideological, religious and so on. In fact any relationship between two or more people involves some element of power — husband and wife, teacher and pupil, employer and employee.

Usually, however, the concept of power is used in a narrower sense, in analysis of POLITICAL power, in the relationships between rulers and ruled in such systems of government as dictatorship and democracy (see p. 22). Within sociology different perspectives tend to hold very different views of power:

1 Weberians tend to see power as the ability of an individual or group of individuals to control, oppress and exploit others in their own interests.

2 Marxists also see power as a source of social conflict but for them it is independent of particular individuals. Rather it is based on the class structure of society; it is the ability of one class to control others and such power rests ultimately on its control of the means of production (see MARXISM, p. 61).

3 Functionalist writers, like the American Talcott Parsons, see power in a much more consensual way, not as power over others for sectional interests but as something possessed by society as a whole and used for the general good or common aims. Through elections politicians are given the authority to carry out such goals. Should they fail, the electorate can dismiss them.

Such perspectives are reflected in the ongoing debate within sociology between PLURALISTS and ELITISTS over the distribution of power in advanced industrial societies. In the past the most powerful groups in society actually ruled the country, but today power seems to be widely dispersed and there seems to be a clear separation between political power (the government and the state) and other forms of power (economic, religious, etc.). Moreover it appears that the people, through their elected representatives, rule themselves rather than being dominated and controlled by an elite, as in the past. This is the basis of the PLURALIST view of power today. Pluralists see power in modern societies as dispersed amongst a wide variety of groups from businessmen to unions to boy scouts with no one group dominating. In their view the government acts as a sort of broker, arbitrating between such conflicting interests ultimately in the interest of society at large.

POWER (continued)

Elitists, however, see power in advanced industrial society as highly concentrated in the hands of a few, a power elite or, from a Marxist perspective, a ruling class who use the government to promote their own interest and preserve their wealth and privilege. Advocates of these two theories not only disagree over the structure of power but over the best way to define and measure it. Whilst pluralists tend to concentrate on 'actual' power, on government actions and decisions, elitists have looked at 'potential' power — at the social and educational background of top decision-makers, at economic and ideological power as well as at government and at the distribution of wealth. Thus whilst pluralist studies in Great Britain, like Christopher Hewitt's and Arnold Rose's ('Elites and the Distribution of Power in British Society in P. Stanworth and A. Giddens (eds), *Elites and Power in British Society*, 1974) and in America (*The Power Structure*, 1967) show that no one group in recent years has had paramount influence over government decisions, Marxists like C.W. Mills (*The Power Elite*, 1956) have sought to show how the political, business and military elites are interlinked, how Parliament acts as a committee of the bourgeoisie (Ralph Milliband, *The State of Capitalist Society*, 1969) and how through NON-DECISION MAKING (Barach & Baratz, *The Two Faces of Power*, 1962) the powerful prevent key issues such as poverty, race and the distribution of wealth ever getting on to the political agenda. The poor, the weak and the radical are simply excluded from decision-making.

Moreover, as Stephen Lukes (*Power: A Radical View*, 1974) argues, real power is the ability to get others to want what you want them to want and here ideological power is crucial. This power over people's ideas, over the framework of public discussions, this ability to get the masses to accept the existing social system as not only inevitable but natural and just, was highlighted in the University of Glasgow Media Group's study of the way both the BBC and ITV portrayed the 'News' (*Bad News, More Bad News* and *Really Bad News*). Despite the official claims of neutrality and impartiality, the Media Group claimed to have found a consistant 'pro-Establishment' bias in News broadcasts. Radical ideas and personalities were either excluded or 'smeared'.

Whilst liberal and pluralist writers, especially in America, tend to see modern democracy as both effective and fair, Marxists argue that only with the advent of socialism and the communal ownership of the means of production will true democracy ever exist. In their view political liberty is impossible without economic equality. Such a debate highlights the huge variety of ways of defining, measuring and analysing POWER.

See also DEMOCRACY, ELITE.

is for
PROFESSIONS

the higher professions — judges, doctors, scientists, engineers. Those with less independence, self-regulation and lower pay and status are called the lower professions. These include teachers, social workers and nurses — but even these groups enjoy greater social prestige, security and career prospects than skilled manual workers, even if their pay is similar.

The members of the professions are characterised by trust and respect — our trust in their professional judgement, our belief that they will only act in the interests of their client and the community at large. In return we accord them high status and (to some of them) generous

The professions have been one of the biggest areas of occupational growth in advanced industrial societies in recent years. This is due not only to an expansion of the traditional professions, but also the growth of new ones serving modern government — teachers, nurses, town planners and so on. The skills and knowledge of professionals are seen as essential for the development and expansion of modern economies, and the wealth these economies produce helps to pay for their services.

So what makes a job into a profession? Geoffrey Millerson in *The Qualifying Associations* (1964) has outlined the following key ingredients:

Skill based on theoretical knowledge
The skill requires training and education
The professional must demonstrate competence by passing a test
Integrity is maintained by adherence to a code of conduct
The service is for the public good
The profession is organised

Professionals who fulfil all these criteria are members of what are usually termed

financial reward. Functionalist writers since Emile Durkheim have put particular faith in such groups as the means to ensuring efficiency in the social system, 'organic' solidarity and maintaining ethical standards.

However, this image has become increasingly tarnished in recent years. The Austrian educationalist Ivan Illich, in particular, has criticised what he sees as the threat to society and the individual from the growth and power of the professions. He has called for a 'deschooling of society' to liberate children's capacity to learn. He also considers the medical profession 'a major threat to health' because of its emphasis on expensive and specialised treatment, rather than on preventing ill-health. In his view the professions are creating a dependency whose main function is to maintain their authority and income, rather than to help people become independent and free.

Radical and Marxist writers go further. They see the professions as an integral part of the ruling class serving the needs of the bourgeoisie. However, by appearing to be acting in the public interest they act as a ▶

PROFESSIONS (continued)

buffer, deflecting criticism from the real controllers of capitalist societies and making the system seem fair and natural. As C. Wright Mills has argued, though the legal profession in America claims to work equally well for all, lawyers have increasingly become the servants of the large corporations, teaching them how to manipulate the law in their own interests (tax evasion, property speculation, etc.). There thus seem to be two 'laws' in America, one for the rich and one for the poor. Terry Johnson and Noel and Jose Parry see professionalism as a strategy for promoting self-interest, a form of trade-unionism masquerading under the guise of public service. Thus Ben David commented in 1964, 'control of entry into the medical societies boosts the incomes of doctors out of all proportion to that of comparable professions, the same way as monopoly profit'. The client rarely has the opportunity for criticism or recompense. As the *Report on Professional Services* by the Monopolies Commission in 1970 concluded, 'a number of the restrictive practices carried on by professional groups looked ... rather like arrangements for making life easier for practitioners at the expense of their clients'.

Despite such criticism, society seems to be becoming increasingly specialised as more and more occupations seek to join the ranks of the professions. Newcomers include osteopaths, physiotherapists and even undertakers (funeral directors). Unable to afford such expensive services, some developing countries have adopted the non-professional approach. The best-known example, perhaps, is China's 'barefoot doctors'.

See also MIDDLE CLASS.

nature of capitalist society, they would be transformed from being a 'class in itself' to being one 'for itself'. As the underlying contradictions in the capitalist mode of production reached crisis point, the proletariat would rise up, overthrow the bourgeoisie and establish a 'Dictatorship of the Proletariat', a transitory period from capitalism to socialism and communism during which the last remnants of bourgeois rule would be eliminated, state ownership and management of the economy would be established and the workers would be educated into true freedom, justice and self-government.

The main problem for Marxist writers since, though, has been that far from polarising into two classes, advanced

is for
PROLETARIAT

PB

Originally, the term proletariat referred to the lowest social class in ancient Rome, but was later used derogatively about people in the lowest social class anywhere. It gained precise and universal meaning when it was adopted by Karl Marx to refer to industrial workers in capitalist societies.

Marx believed that capitalist societies would increasingly polarise into two major classes: the bourgeoisie − those owning the means of production; and the proletariat − the mass of workers with nothing to sell, save their own labour. Exploited by the businessmen in their pursuit of profit the working classes would be reduced to subsistence wages but would grow in size as petty-bourgeois elements (e.g. small businesses, clerks, executives) were also driven into wage labour by 'monopoly capital' (companies controlling single industries, multinationals, big banks) and would develop class consciousness through the factory system, trade unionism and the 'education' and leadership of the Communist Party. As the workers came to recognise the exploitative and oppressive

capitalist societies have developed a third − a middle class. And instead of working-class consciousness solidifying, it still seems as fragmented as ever. David Lockwood, for example, has identified three distinctive types of working class:

The PROLETARIAN workers with a conflict view of the social structure and strong support for trade unions (dockers, miners)
The DEFERENTIAL worker with a hierarchical, harmonious view of society, often votes Conservative (agricultural workers, workers in small businesses, older workers)
PRIVATISED workers − identified by Goldthorpe and Lockwood's Luton study as adopting an "instrumental" attitude to work, society and the unions and Labour party in their pursuit of affluence.

As Frank Parkin has argued, the majority of the working class have either absorbed the dominant values of capitalism or at least accepted them as inevitable. Marxists, however, argue that such workers suffer ▶

PROLETARIAT (continued)

from 'false consciousness'. They have been duped by the media and tempted by the false promises of the advertising man. They have yet to recognise their true position as victims of a system that robs them not only of the real value of their labour but of a sense of human dignity and worth. As Westergaard and Resler argue, the predominant feeling of the working class is 'a common sense of grievance', a belief that the dice is 'loaded against ordinary workers'. They know the existing social order is wrong but not why or what they can do about it. As the crisis of capitalism develops, their instrumental attitudes can all too easily turn into revolutionary ones as their affluence is hit by low wages and redundancies.

In their search for the 'inevitable crisis of capitalism' amid the depression of the 1970s several Marxist writers have put forward the proletarianisation thesis. According to this, rather than affluent workers becoming middle-class, the lower middle classes are descending into the working class, economically and psychologically.

Thus, J. Westergaard and H. Resler have claimed: 'If routine non-manual work is bracketed with manual work, with which it now has so many conditions in common, at least three in every four men and five in every six women are in jobs of an essentially wage-earning character – male clerks and shopworkers are now firmly among the broad mass of ordinary labour.'

The factory-like conditions of modern office-work and the growth of white-collar trade unionism are taken as signs of the proletarianisation of clerks, secretaries and the service occupations. As their incomes have declined and as they too experience increasing control from above, there is now little to distinguish them from skilled manual workers.

The American Marxist Harry Braverman has gone further. By defining the proletariat as 'that class which possessing nothing but its power to labour, sells that power in return for its subsistence' he includes in its ranks 70% of the US labour force. Modern capitalism, he argues, is characterised by control from above. Automation and rationalisation have 'DESKILLED' the modern worker and so made him replaceable and easy to control whilst he in turn depends on capitalism for his good services and standard of living. Further, the bulk of the US labour force is now employed by private industry or its agent, the state. Thus in his view such intermediate classes as lower management, technicians and state employees 'bear the mark of the proletarian condition'. Despite their 'petty share in the prerogatives and rewards of capital' and their authority over lesser workers, such groups are also exploited. However, they have yet to recognise this.

It is exactly this lack of class-consciousness that has formed the major criticism of the proletarianisation thesis. As David Lockwood argues, clerks are neither middle nor working-class. Ken Roberts's study of such 'middle classes' in Liverpool (*The Fragmentary Class Structure*, 1977) and Wilmott and Young's in Woodford Green (*Family and Class in a London Suburb*, 1960) all show self-conscious bourgeois views. In no way do they identify with the working class. Rather their form of trade unionism is a defensive strategy to preserve their status and differentials against affluent workers, not a means to uniting with them. The 1979 and especially 1983 elections showed a lack of class-consciousness and militancy even against a right-wing Tory government and mass unemployment of three million. False consciousness, the power of the media and innate British conservatism may be part of the answer but not all of it.

See also EMBOURGEOISEMENT, MARXISM, WORKING CLASS.

is for
PSEPHOLOGY

born to rule. Such voters tend to have a rather hierarchical view of society. Secular voters tend to adopt a pragmatic view of politics and simply see the Tory Party as containing the more able and experienced politicians.

2 The embourgeoisement thesis, put forward by Ferdinand Zweig in the early 1960s, stated that the more affluent members of the working class were becoming middle-class in their lifestyle and attitudes and so in their voting behaviour. Goldthorpe and Lockwood's study of Luton car workers largely disproved this theory, though it has seen some revival in recent years (see p. 30).

Psephology is the word used to describe the study of elections. It is derived from *psiphos*, the pebble which the Athenians dropped into an urn to vote. Elections are the key aspect of democratic political systems and so of immense interest, not only to politicians but to academics and journalists.

Electoral studies have shown that traditionally the major influence on political attitudes and voting behaviour in Britain is social class – most of the middle class vote Conservative, most of the working class vote Labour. Why, you might ask, doesn't Labour win every general election, since almost 50% of the electorate is working-class? A psephologist would answer that this is because a third of the working class votes Conservative, and it is part of his job to find out why. Explanations for such cross-class voting include:

1 The deferential-secular thesis, put forward by E.A. Nordinger in *Working Class Tories* (1967) and by R. McKenzie and A. Silver, in *Angels in Marble* (1968): deferential voters prefer politicians of a high social status, those

3 The importance of a voter's age and generation. Once voting allegiances are formed they rarely change and, as D. Butler and D. Stokes noted, a large percentage of working-class Tories are older voters, and when they first voted there was no Labour Party.

4 The importance of environment and region. Friends, neighbourhood and so on can influence the way people behave. In the 1960s and 1970s the electoral map of Britain showed certain areas to be solidly Labour (for instance, South Wales) while others contained a high percentage of working-class Tories (Blackpool, for example).

There are in contrast few studies of what Frank Parkin called 'middle-class radicals', those from middle-class backgrounds who vote Labour (about 20% of the middle class). Such voters tend to come from the 'caring professions' – teaching, social work, etc., and see the Labour Party's view of justice as a fairer one than the Conservative.

Similarly they and other government employees have a vested interest in ▶

returning the party most likely to expand government services and spending since this will increase their job security and promotion prospects. Alternatively, those from working-class backgrounds who have risen into the middle classes often retain their traditional voting habits and so continue to vote Labour. Other factors, such as a person's age, sex or religion, tend to be more marginal influences.

This was the traditional picture of voting behaviour in Britain in the 1950s and 1960s. Party, habit and predictability were the main characteristics. The 1970s and 1980s, in particular the General Elections of 1979 and 1983, have led to a dramatic reassessment. Studies like Ivor Crewe's and Bo Salik's *A Decade of Dealignment* (1983), David Butler and Dennis Kavanagh's *The British General Election of 1979* (1980) and Richard Rose's *Class Does Not Equal Party* (Strathclyde University Occasional Papers) all reveal that:

(a) Social class is no longer such a dominant influence on the way people vote. The traditional link of class and party is less strong. Mrs Thatcher's victories in both 1979 and 1983 owed a lot to support from skilled workers in the South East and nearly 30% of the unemployed voted for her in 1983. The last General Election was Labour's worst defeat ever (only 28% of the vote). According to Ivor Crewe, the majority of manual workers voted Tory, SDP or did not vote and this severely undermined Labour's claim to be the party of the working class. For the first time more men voted Tory than women.

(b) The ELECTORATE is increasingly VOLATILE, less predictable, less stable and less class-conscious. Issues and personalities now have greater influence than habit and the FLOATING VOTE (those uncommitted to any major party) has grown. The Falklands factor, the con-trasting images of Mrs Thatcher and Mr Foot, the influence of the media and party propaganda, the divisions between right and left in the Labour Party, all had a great influence.

(c) The DECLINE of the traditional TWO-PARTY SYSTEM. In 1951 the two major parties shared 97% of the vote between them. By 1983 this had fallen to 70.6% due to the rise of THIRD PARTIES, in particular the Social Democratic-Liberal Alliance which gained 26% of the vote in 1983, compared with 28% for Labour and 43% for the Conservatives. However, due to the distorting effect of our FIRST-PAST-THE-POST SYSTEM (the CUBE EFFECT), *inside* Parliament Labour and Conservative still dominate. Mrs Thatcher, with virtually the same percentage of the vote as in 1979, got 100 more seats in the House of Commons and though Labour only had 2% more votes than the SDP Alliance it got 209 seats and the Alliance only 23. Under PRO-PORTIONAL REPRESENTATION, the Tories would have got 280 seats, Labour 182, and the SDP Alliance 170.

(d) REGIONALISM is now a much greater influence, and a fairly clear division of the country into Labour and Conservative areas is evident. Whilst Labour controls the North, Scotland and Wales, the South and South East are almost totally Tory with a spread of Alliance pockets. In 1983 Labour won only three seats outside London in the whole of the South East of England and was driven back to its heartlands in the traditional industrial areas and inner cities.

This changing electoral pattern reflects certain underlying social changes:

(i) A changing occupational structure. As white-collar, non-manual jobs grow, manual ones are shrinking.

(ii) A significant migration of population from the industrial North to the pro-sperous South as traditional industries decline.

(iii) Mass unemployment has led not only

to a fall in trade union membership but in militant attitudes. Fear for one's job overrides demands for radical change.

(iv) Growth in home ownership (approx 63% of the population), encouraged by the Conservative policy of selling council houses, has led to more 'conservative' attitudes and a shrinking council-house population, one of Labour's key areas of support.

(v) An ageing population (9.5 million, nearly 18% of the population) which generally benefits the Conservatives.

American studies show a similarly volatile picture with issues, personalities and media images very influential. However, only 50-60% voted in the 1980 and 1984 presidential elections, a sign of possible disillusion.

In both countries, therefore, short-term influences are crucial to winning modern elections. One particular influence has been the OPINION POLL surveys of public opinion on major political issues, which attempt to predict how people will vote. Such surveys have developed from purely academic exercises into big business. Opinion polls can be very accurate — but with the closeness of post-war elections even a small percentage error can ruin a prediction. Equally, such polls can have some influence on the result.

One theory as to why Harold Wilson lost the 1970 election was that all the polls predicted a Labour landslide, and as a result many Labour voters didn't bother to turn out. In some countries, such as West Germany, opinion polls are banned in the period before a general election.

However, sociologists and psephologists differ in their views as to the value and function of modern elections:

1 Liberal and functionalist writers tend to see them as the 'arteries' of modern democracy, as the main means by which our leaders are chosen and kept in check, by which the electorate communicate their views and CONSENT to the party in power. Power is thus legitimised.

2 Radical, especially Marxist writers, see elections more as a puppet show to divert the people, give them an appearance of choice and yet leave real power in the hands of the ruling class. Whilst difficult to prove in Western democracies, such mass manipulation is very evident in such one-party states as the USSR and in many Third World countries.

See also DEMOCRACY, ELITES, POWER.

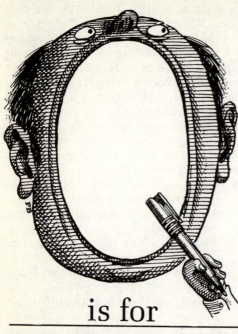

is for

QUESTIONNAIRES

tentions. Obviously once such questions go beyond purely factual answers, they must be as clear, precise and unambiguous as possible. For example, the question 'Do you read a lot?' is open to all sorts of interpretations. To some people, one or two books a year is a lot. It would be better to phrase the question thus: 'How many books a month do you read on average?' and give a set of number ranges to choose from.

Social surveys are usually of two types:

1 descriptive — to measure, say, the extent of poverty
2 analytical — seeking explanations of, say, the relationship between voting behaviour and such variables as social class, age, sex and religion. Depending, then, on the type of information required, questionnaires may be either:

Questionnaires come in all shapes and sizes from postcards to multi-page documents. They are lists of pre-set questions to which people are asked to supply answers. Most social surveys use questionnaires because they are a relatively cheap, fast and efficient method of obtaining a large amount of information about a large number of people in a short space of time.

Usually questionnaires are given to only a sample of the people from whom information is sought. For instance, a survey on voting intentions does not mean that every voter has to be interviewed. The cost in terms of time and money would be enormous: the only nationwide survey is the census and even this is only conducted every ten years and at government expense.

Questionnaires can be used to ask questions on a whole range of topics from voting behaviour to religious attitudes, from leisure activities to purchasing in-

(a) open-ended — where respondents supply their own answers
(b) closed/fixed-choice types — where the answers are already given and the respondent merely says 'yes' or 'no' and ticks one of a list of alternative answers.

Fixed-choice answers are obviously much easier to classify, code and quantify but they do not allow respondents to explain their views fully or to develop their answers. Open-ended questions do have this advantage, and so provide a truer, more valid picture of people's opinions, though it is a vaguer and less precise one.

Equally important is the method used to administer the questionnaire — in person or by post. Again the key considerations are not only time and cost but the 'depth' to which the questions intend to go:

1 Delivery by trained interviewers ensures that the right person answers

and that the whole of the questionnaire is completed, fully understood and truthfully answered. However, not only is this method expensive but it also introduces the problem of INTER-VIEWER-BIAS, the possibility that by the way he or she asks the questions, codes the answers or even dresses, the interviewer will influence the answers given.

2 Postal questionnaires avoid this problem and are a cheap method of reaching a wide range of people, especially over a large area. However, this technique often suffers from a low RESPONSE-RATE, possibly as low as 20%. The lower the response-rate the less valid the survey since the replies represent only a small percentage of the sample and a biased one at that, biased towards those committed enough to respond. There is also no guarantee that the questions have been fully understood or that the right person filled it in. Someone else in the household may have answered it or it may have been a 'group' effort. To encourage a good response-rate such surveys often use authoritative covering letters, stamped, addressed reply envelopes, various prizes or inducements and/or follow-ups by trained interviewers.

Surveys, therefore, require considerable thought and planning and usually a PILOT STUDY is conducted beforehand – a sort of dress rehearsal to eliminate possible errors. Such surveys have proved extremely popular in sociology, especially amongst positivist sociologists (see p. 78) as the main means to establish 'facts and figures' about society today. Phenomenologists (see p. 75), however, dispute not only the reliability of such a technique (its accuracy) but its VALIDITY, its ability to truthfully represent respondents' views. By the way they are worded and by the way they are asked, questions can as easily 'create' answers as elicit them. They can 'lead' the respondent towards a particular answer, by being vague, ambiguous or hypothetical. They can produce false answers, by asking difficult questions or ones which rely on memory. They can cause people to put down the first thing they think of, and on sensitive issues such as religion, or sexual habits people often lie or at least exaggerate.

Add to this, problems of interviewer-bias and the sociologist's own need to establish (or impose) some sort of order and pattern on a mass of varied replies and you can see why phenomenologists 'question' such questionnaires. Despite their drawbacks, however, questionnaire surveys are widely used, not only by sociologists but also by government and market-research firms. If carefully designed and handled, they can provide a vast array of information. Their validity and reliability decrease as the questions move from factual to motivational issues, and they are accurate only at the time of the survey.

See also SAMPLING.

is for
ROLE

Role is one of the smallest yet most basic terms in the sociological dictionary since it provides a bridge between our behaviour as individuals and as members of groups or society at large.

In any situation involving two or more people there will be certain behaviour that is expected. For instance, we expect all policemen, doctors or teachers to act in a certain way. They, in turn, can expect a certain response from us. A doctor expects cooperation from his patients, a teacher from his pupils. A social role thus involves mutual expectations, otherwise the whole set of role relationships upon which society is founded will collapse.

Social roles can be divided into formal (judge, priest, milkman) and informal (father, son, friend), but no individual plays only one role in society. Most of us perform a variety of multiple roles. The local bank manager may also be chairman of the ratepayers' association or the golf club, for instance.

The term role-set is more specific and refers to the way one of these major roles brings an individual into direct relationships with others. A local doctor's role-set would include his relationships with his patients, doctors in the local hospital, fellow doctors in his professional association and so on.

Inevitably, such variety and interconnection of expected ways of behaving involves the possibility of role conflict, either for:

> The individual — the military chaplain, say, who is both an officer and a priest. Between individuals, in the performance of their expected roles — the engineer and the production manager clashing over quality versus quantity, for example.

As we grow up, we learn roles as part of the socialisation process. We acquire the norms, values and roles expected by society both by observing and imitating adults — especially our parents — and by a system of rewards and punishments. A dutiful son is praised, a naughty pupil is punished.

Equally a doctor who commits misconduct with a patient is struck off, a hard-working manager is promoted. Such sanctions can be quite minor or informal but nevertheless effective — a stern look, 'being sent to Coventry', idle gossip, for example.

It appears at times as though social roles control everything we do, and there has been a great deal of sociological controversy about this.

Functionalist writers, like Talcott Parsons, have put so much emphasis on social roles and socialisation that they make people seem to be little more than puppets 'jumping about on the end of an invisible string, cheerfully acting out their assigned parts', as Peter Berger has put it.

In contrast, interactionists like G.H. Mead have put greater emphasis on individuals and their ability to interpret roles according to their own ideas and the meanings they give to the behaviour of others. Rather than viewing society as determining how such roles are to be performed, interactionists see social roles as vague and ambiguous – an open script that provides broad guidelines, but leaves the individual actor with considerable scope for improvisation and creativity. For example, some teachers see their role more as one of 'law and order' than of teaching. Similarly, role-relationships are not seen as pre-determined but open to negotiation as, say, in a fairly open and democratic marriage. From such a perspective the individual is seen as a conscious actor capable of self-awareness and even of 'taking the role' of the other. We expect doctors to wear white coats and vicars 'dog collars' and we cooperate more willingly when they fulfil these expectations. Erving Goffman has extended this form of analysis into a study of the 'presentation of the self' and the concept of role distance; people's ability to free themselves from playing social roles in an entirely predictable way. We learn to put on a 'front' to create a particular image or response as a means to increasing or gaining control of a situation; for example, a policeman who cracks jokes. Such strategies are learnt and developed throughout life in particular by children in ROLE PLAY. Here by playing Mummy and Daddy or Doctor and Nurse they not only learn how to play a particular social part but how to handle the reactions and demands of others.

Nevertheless social roles do have a very powerful influence on our behaviour, in particular GENDER ROLES – our expectations about how boys or girls should behave and look. Such roles are 'ascribed' (determined by birth) rather than achieved and they are basic in the sense that they are not related to any particular job or situation but pervade all aspects of life. Sex roles dominate people's lives, women's in particular, influencing not only whether they can go to work but what types of job are open to them. The working mother faces the classic dilemma of role-conflict, and feminist writers have made the idea of a woman's place not being in the home a central focus of their campaign to 'liberate' women.

The concept of ROLE is thus a crucial one in sociology, though with the decline in influence of both functionalism and interactionism a less significant one in the theories of the 1980s.

See also NORMS, GROUP.

is for
SAMPLING

One of the key stages in any social survey is the selection of the group of people to be studied or interviewed — what sociologists call the 'population', be it housewives or OAPs. In some cases it may be possible to interview every member of the 'population' under investigation because it is such a small group (say cabinet ministers), or because the organisation involved has the time and the resources for a full-scale survey (for example, the government and its census every ten years). However, because of cost and time, most surveys are limited to interviewing a sample — and it is vital that the sample selected should be as representative as possible. The more

accurate and representative the sample the more valid the responses, and so the conclusions, are likely to be.

The stages of sampling are:

1 Defining the 'population' – deciding exactly which group of people the researcher aims to interview
2 Finding a suitable 'sampling frame' (a list of the group of people to be surveyed) such as the Electoral Register
3 Deciding on the SAMPLE SIZE or 'FRACTION'. This obviously depends on the amount of time and money available; normally in the region of 1–3000 people for a national survey. Too small a sample (e.g. below 100 people) makes it difficult to calculate SAMPLING ERROR or the extent to which the sample is a reasonable representation of the 'population' involved.
4 Deciding on a SAMPLING METHOD.
   (a) One method commonly used is quota sampling, where the sample chosen is a 'mirror-reflection' of the population under investigation. For example, in a survey of pensioners' attitudes to the health service the interviewer would try to choose the correct proportions of men and women of newly-retired and very old, of those of middle and working-class backgrounds, of those on state pensions only and those on private ones, and so on.

   Quota sampling is widely used in market research surveys because it is cheap and easy to administer. But its reliability is limited because: (i) All the chief characteristics of a given 'population' are rarely accurately known, and (ii) much depends on the expertise and honesty of the interviewers.
   (b) A more widely used and more scientific method is random sampling. This form of sampling is based on probability theory and its various mathematical formulae.

Using this method, it is possible to calculate within a specified range of accuracy, the chances that a sample randomly chosen is typical of the 'population' under study, because each member of that 'population' has an equal chance of being selected.

Here interviewers are not involved in selecting whom to interview. They are simply presented with a list of people selected, and cannot interview anyone else. Should they not be able to contact some of the sample, complicated procedures have to be gone through if substitutes are allowed. A simple random sample would thus consist of putting all the names of the group involved in a hat and drawing out, say, fifty of them. A more systematic random sample would consist of selecting names at regular intervals, say every tenth or hundredth, from some predetermined list such as the electoral register or certain medical lists.

For a more accurate or detailed analysis it may be possible to stratify the 'population' involved into certain sections or strata. For example it may be known that 25 per cent of all pensioners are male and 75 per cent female. The sample chosen can then be divided correspondingly and each sub-sample selected randomly or by quota.

Alternatively the 'population' involved may live in CLUSTERS and so it may save time and money to select a sample of such clusters and select sub-samples from them (randomly or by quota) as for example in surveys of NHS patients (in hospitals) or council tenants (high-rise blocks). Cluster sampling is not so scientifically accurate as other methods but makes up for this by increasing the possibility of getting the whole sample to answer the questionnaire

(c) However, in most large-scale inquiries, especially when the 'population' is widely dispersed, some form of MULTI-STAGE SAMPLING is used. A sample of first-stage units is selected and each of these is sub-sampled. For example, the first stage in a national survey may be constituencies, then wards, then households.

The adoption of probability theory and the use of computer techniques have greatly increased the accuracy and reliability of modern surveys. Thus a well-chosen sample of 2500 people can effectively represent the whole population of Great Britain. Though 'scientific' sampling only dates from the turn of the century, it is widely used today in all forms of social investigation – by sociologists, government departments, market researchers and opinion polls. The more accurate the sample, the more reliable and valid the answers – though this also depends on the validity of the QUESTIONNAIRE (see p. 90).

see p. 90

OXFORD ST.

is for
SECTS

Religious sects fascinate sociologists not only because they are an exception to the general rule that religion in advanced industrial societies is in decline, but also because such groups often seem to be on the 'margins' of society.

Newspapers often tell of the scandalous activities of some fringe group or another, whether it is the 'brainwashing' of the Moonies or the mass suicides discovered at the People's Temple in Guyana. Nevertheless, it is estimated that about five per cent of the adult population in Britain belong to sects of some kind and however strange they may appear, sects obviously fulfil some need that normal society doesn't.

A sect is usually defined as a com-paratively small group of individuals aspiring to personal perfection in the religious sense. Such groups are usually highly exclusive. Strict conformity to a particular code of behaviour is enforced and the purity of the group maintained by occasional expulsions. Membership of a sect comes to dominate a member's life-style, and may include rejection of society at large and all previous relations and loyalties – or even names. Members of a sect often see themselves as the chosen few, an elect. They distrust normal society and, in particular, reject the 'corrupted teaching' of established religions. They key characteristics of a sect can therefore be summed up as:

Elitism – their self-concept as an elect, the chosen few.
Authoritarianism – their belief that their creed alone is the 'Truth and the Way'. Criticism is forbidden.
Totalitarianism – their demand for total adherence to its beliefs and way of life. No other loyalty is tolerated.

Sects tend to rise during periods of rapid social change. The Oxford sociologist Bryan Wilson has seen the rise of Methodism as a response of the new urban working class to the chaos and uncertainty of life in newly-settled industrial areas in the seventeenth century. In the midst of upheaval, sect life offers stability, a sense of community and purpose. As Max Weber argued, sects also appeal to those groups which are marginal in society, particularly the poor. Pentecostalist sects, for instance, have been popular among West Indian immigrants in Britain.

Feelings of economic and social inferiority can be compensated for by a sense of religious superiority; a sort of 'theodicy of disprivilege', as Weber called it. The idea is that the deprivations of this world will be replaced by riches and honours in the next.

In *Sects and Society* (1961) Bryan Wilson categorised sects according to their main objectives:

the *conversionist* sect, which seeks to alter people

the *adventist* sect, which seeks to change the world

the *introversionist* sect, which seeks to replace worldly values by higher inner personal values

the *gnostic* sect, which more or less accepts the standards of society but seeks to achieve social goals by mystical means.

In a later work (*Religious Sects*, 1970) he added other categories such as the Utopian sects which withdraw from the world in order to construct a new model upon which it can be rebuilt. According to H. Richard Niebuhr (*The Social Sources of Denominationalism*, 1929) most sects are short-lived because the fervour and commitment of their members rarely survives the founding generation. Members grow older and/or wealthier and re-enter mainstream society, or the sect grows into a denomination and so appeals to a wider audience. Its radical preaching either becomes part of accepted social wisdom, or is no longer relevant to a changing society. A sect thus thrives or dies, though some have managed to remain sect-like, for example the Mormons and Jehovah Witnesses.

In the sociology of religion it is important to distinguish sects from other religious groups and organisations, in particular:

DENOMINATION — minority religions that often originally were sects. Membership is usually voluntary and open and their teachings usually tolerate and recognise other 'visions' of the truth. Usually such organisations only survive in fairly tolerant and pluralistic societies or else they would be driven underground by the Established Church or the state.

CHURCHES — religious organisations with a hierarchy of paid officials which seek to minister to the whole of society. A Church usually identifies with the state and supports the general norms and values of society. It is thus usually part of the Establishment and so more the mouthpiece of the wealthy than the poor. It seeks to be INCLUSIVE (compare with the exclusiveness of sects) in the way it claims a monopoly of religious truth and to speak for all in society (e.g the Church of England).

See also SECULARISATION, GROUPS.

1 The decline in religious practice and participation in advanced industrial societies. Britain, for example, is reputed to be the most secular nation in Europe. In 1950 two-thirds of the children born alive in England were baptised in the Church of England; by 1970 this figure was well under half. On average only 10-15 per cent of adults attend church on Sundays.

2 The decline in religious belief. In affluent western societies religion has become a minority interest among the many other intellectual, cultural and social pursuits. In the view of the American sociologist, Peter Berger, people in the west increasingly 'look upon the world and their own lives without the benefit of religious interpretations' and are experiencing a secularisation of consciousness as the search for material prosperity has replaced that for religious truth.

3 The decline of the church as a major social institution. Many of the church's social functions have been taken over by secular institutions. Science now explains the previously unexplainable and can even produce test tube babies. The welfare state cares for people 'from the cradle to the grave' and educates our children. The newspaper and the

is for
SECULARISATION

One of the neatest definitions of secularisation comes from the Oxford sociologist Bryan Wilson. He calls it the process through which religious thinking, practice and institutions 'lose their social significance'. The idea owes much to Max Weber's theory that as society became increasingly industrialised, rational and scientific ideas would sweep away traditional and irrational sources of authority and belief like religion. The secularisation idea rests on four main arguments:

television are the modern pulpits. The power of churchmen today seems insignificant compared to the power of a Cardinal Wolsey.

4 Secularisation within the church. In the Roman Catholic church, for example, the Mass is now in English rather than Latin, and many denominations have amalgamated or are proposing to do so. As Bryan Wilson comments: 'Organisations amalgamate when they are weak rather than when they are strong,

since alliance means compromise and amendments of commitment.'

However, there are many criticisms of this thesis:

(a) Like all statistics, those on religion are open to alternative interpretation. For instance, few people in Britain today attend church, yet surveys have shown up to 90 per cent of people claiming to believe in God, and 60 per cent claiming to belong to the Anglican church.

(b) Even if they are valid, the statistics prove little about the depth of religious beliefs. Studies have shown that most people in Britain do not necessarily equate church-going with religious conviction. The decline in the RANGE of the church's functions does not necessarily mean that the church today has no function to play. In his analysis of America, Talcott Parsons sees the churches as more specialised, professional and so stronger. Religious (especially Christian) attitudes and ethics still underlie American society. David Martin argues the same about Britain.

(c) The growth of religious sects, especially in so advanced a society as America, where today nearly two-thirds of the population claim membership of a religious body. As Robert Bellah argues, what has changed is the method of worship – sects rather than churches – not the need to. Others, like Peter Berger, however, see this religious revival as merely another example of American commercialism, as 'TV religion'. Such sects only add to the disintegration of American society.

(d) There never was a 'Golden Age' for Religion to decline from. There never was a Church of America and even in Victorian Britain only 40% of the adult population regularly attended church according to the 1851 census and these were mainly from the upper and middle classes – for social as much as religious reasons.

(e) The problem of establishing cause and effect, of establishing whether secularisation was caused by industrialisation or whether, as Max Weber argued, the Protestant ethic sparked off the Industrial Revolution.

So varied are the uses of this term, so different the interpretations given to the facts and figures involved, that David Martin has argued for the removal of the word secularisation from the sociological 'dictionary'. Certainly the two sides in this debate often seem to be talking about different things – the decline of ORGANISED RELIGION versus the continued strength of INDIVIDUAL CONVICTION. Whilst secularisation may be occurring in advanced Protestant countries, is it really happening everywhere else (Northern Ireland, Iran, the Lebanon, modern Spain, etc.)?

See also SECTS.

is for SOCIAL ANTHRO- POLOGY

Anthropology is usually defined in dictionaries as 'the study of humankind'. But there's more to it than this. A modern anthropologist, John Beattie, has described the work of social anthropologists as studying 'people's customs, social institutions and values and the ways in which these are interrelated. They carry out their investigations mainly in the context of living communities (usually relatively small-scale ones) and their central, though not their only interest is in systems of social relations' (*Other Cultures*, 1966). The studies of anthropologists have shown that pre-industrial societies, far from being simple or backward are in fact highly complex, with elaborate rituals and cultures.

Early anthropology originated from attempts by nineteenth-century historians like Lewis Morgan and sociologists like Emile Durkheim to categorise societies into general types and establish their historical origins. However, their generalisations were based primarily on accounts of tribal peoples provided by travellers, missionaries and colonial administrators. Modern anthropology is not usually said to have 'taken off' until anthropologists began to undertake their own fieldwork using a relatively scientific approach. An important pioneer was the British anthropologist Bronislaw Malinowski (1884-1942). From 1914 to 1918 Malinowski made detailed studies of the life of the natives of the Trobriand Islands, off New Guinea, which endowed anthropology with a respectability of its own.

Using a functionalist perspective he analysed the Islanders' social systems as a means to surviving in that particular environment and living together as a harmonious community. From such a perspective, every part of the social system had a particular function to play. For example, his study of magic showed that its main function was to relieve anxiety about the unknown and was thus much more than mere superstition.

This 'scientific' approach led to a proliferation of anthropological societies and university departments between the two World Wars. By the 1960s the functionalist model was, however, being increasingly criticised for being too static a view, for being unable to explain social change. The social anthropology of the 1960s was increasingly influenced by the structuralist theories of Claude Lévi-Strauss, with their emphasis on language as the key distinction between societies. To structuralists, culture represents more than just language and rituals; it is an expression of the human unconscious, man's inner psyche. By tracing the roots of languages and cultures, Lévi-Strauss claimed to be able to link the rules of kinship and marriage of, say, the Australian aborigine with that of the North Buram Kachin. By the 1970s this approach too was under criticism as being too ambitious for the methodology at present available. One attempt to overcome such limitations was that of structural Marxists. Thus social anthropology has moved from the 'cultural relativism' of Malinowski and Radcliffe-Brown, that societies could only be analysed in their own terms, to approaches seeking to establish general or universal principles of social structure and change.

The methodology of this particular social science is crucial because of the problems of evaluating other societies in western terms. The basis of anthropological methodology is fieldwork, a highly detailed analysis of every aspect of a tribe's life and society by, wherever possible, actually participating in its daily life. The idea is to gain insights into why the subjects act as they do and to see the world from their point of view.

However, such participant observation also has considerable 'scientific' dangers, because it relies so heavily on the skill, objectivity, even honesty of a single observer, and there have been numerous examples of studies where information was distorted or made to fit some preconceived theory. For example, early studies of the American Indian tribe, the Zuni, described them as extremely peaceful and harmonious; later ones highlighted the extent of conflict and anxiety manifested in their witchcraft trials. Margaret Mead's famous studies of tribes in New Guinea, which provided a wealth of material about socialisation and sex roles (see GENDER, p. 42) have recently been extensively criticised by Professor Freeman. He found little evidence of the harmony and 'free love' Mead depicted in *Growing Up in New Guinea* and *Coming of Age in Samoa*. The techniques of anthropologists have also been applied to advanced industrial societies. Young and Wilmott's *Family and Kinship in East London* (1957) and Dennis, Henriques and Slaughter's *Coal is Our Life* (1956) are modern examples of detailed fieldwork in small-scale communities. In this sense, anthropology overlaps with other social sciences, particularly sociology – so much so that Professor Raymond Firth has called it 'micro-sociology'.

See also CULTURE, KINSHIP.

Walkies

is for

SOCIAL CONTROL

punish law breakers, but seek to deter others. Should these mechanisms fail, then the army may have to move in – as in Ulster and other societies where law and order have broken down.

But the real basis of control comes from within, from the socialising process we experience as we grow up. From our parents, teachers and employers we learn not only the dangers of misbehaviour and the rewards for doing good – from the smack and the sweet, through to dismissal and promotion – but also the intrinsic satisfaction of self-respect, self-discipline and the feeling of a job well done.

Such socialisation is part and parcel of our preparation for the adult world and roles of parenthood, work and citizenship roles, which in turn are a severe discipline, chaining us down with responsibilities. The irony is that often those with the most power and responsibility have the least

Any social group or organisation has to establish some sort of discipline if order is to be maintained and its members are to perform their functions properly. Such discipline can be either internal or external; it can come from the self-discipline of the members themselves or it can be imposed on them by the rest of the group. Those who persistently reject the group's rules or norms of behaviour may ultimately have to be expelled.

Society at large faces the same basic problems and uses the same basic solutions but on a mass scale, and for an advanced industrial society these problems are even greater because the relationships between its members tend to be more impersonal than those found in small groups or simple societies. Social controls are generally divided into formal and informal ones. The most formal are the police, courts and prisons, who not only catch, judge and

freedom, the least 'time to themselves' – the headmaster, Prime Minister and parent. These formal controls are underpinned by a labyrinth of informal pressures to stop the individual 'stepping out of line' – the 'dirty look', stares, local gossip. However, in a society as diverse and complex as ours, not all such pressures work in the same direction.

Thus, whilst theft is a criminal offence, tax evasion is a national sport; children are taught to tell the truth, while advertisers and politicians are allowed to lie. Similarly the values of a multitude of sub-groups in our society are often in conflict with the social norms.

The most powerful social controls, though, are IDEOLOGICAL ones, the ability to control not only WHAT people think but HOW. Whilst in the past religion performed this function, as the Church controlled people's ideas and ethics, today the media have that power. The question is, who controls the media and in whose interests? Are TV and the newspapers independent as they claim or do they 'make' the news by publishing news they want the public to hear and excluding those they don't?

Such a discussion leads to the debate over who controls the system of social control in modern societies. According to liberal and functionalist writers in a democratic society, the people do. The law and the government are merely expressions of the people's will, made accountable by regular elections. Marxist writers, however, see the police, the courts, the army, the media and even schools as part of the system by which ruling classes in capitalist societies maintain their own power and privilege. Force is rarely used, rather the masses are persuaded to accept the existing social order by having a high standard of living, an apparently free and democratic system of government and a system of mass media that condition them into accepting capitalism as natural and inevitable. Britain is a good example of such 'cultural conditioning'. We are a very conservative people; we dislike rapid social change and radical ideas. Through our history and our socialisation process we have learnt to not only accept but respect those in power over us. Or is our lack of revolutionary fervour even in the midst of mass unemployment simply due to a sense of powerlessness, a feeling that the system cannot be beaten? (see POWER, p. 80, for a fuller discussion of the Elitist/Pluralist debate).

The topic of social control is also inextricably bound up with that of social change. Certainly the breakdown of social solidarity was a central concern to such founding fathers as Emile Durkheim and is of crucial importance to Third World countries today as they too undergo industrialisation. The microchip and mass unemployment have shaken the stability of modern societies and there is today a significant emphasis by politicians and the media on the need to strengthen such social controls as the police and the family. The issue of social control is thus a central one in sociological analyses.

See also IDEOLOGY, POWER, SOCIALISATION.

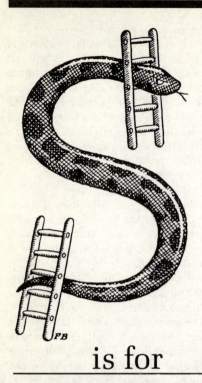

workers, like sales managers and school-teachers

IIIN Skilled non-manual workers, like clerks and shop assistants

IIIM Skilled manual workers, like coal miners

IV Semi-skilled manual workers, like postmen

V Unskilled workers, like dustmen and cleaners.

The main distinction here is between manual and non-manual occupations, usually referred to as the working classes and the middle classes. There are a number of avenues by which *individuals* may move up from one class to another. These include:

- Education and the acquisition of qualifications that will allow entry to a better job
- Marrying someone of a higher social class
- Promotion within a particular

is for

SOCIAL MOBILITY

Social mobility refers to the movement of individuals or groups up and down the social scale. While the social scale in many societies is 'closed and rigid' — as with the caste and feudal systems, for example — the class system in western industrial societies is generally considered to be relatively 'open' and flexible. Consequently, people's social status is not only a matter of birth (ascribed) but may be the result of their own efforts and abilities (achieved).

Such mobility may be either long-range as, say, from social class V to social class IIIM or, as is more usual, short-range — moving up or down by one class on the social scale. The main measure of social class in Britain is that of the Registrar General whose scale is as follows:

I Professional workers, like doctors and lawyers

II Managerial and lower professional

occupation (say, from foreman to manager) or between occupation Individual talent, intelligence and ambition. Here certain fields are more open than others such as sport and entertainment. Kevin Keegan and Rod Stewart are examples of this kind of rise 'from rags to riches'.

Social mobility on a much wider scale may take place through the movement of whole *groups* of individuals. This might happen where there is a substantial change in the occupational structure due to, say, a decline in manual jobs and a growth in white-collar work.

Taking all these factors into account, sociologists have identified three main types of social mobility:

1 Intergenerational mobility — where a

son or daughter achieves a different social position from that of their parents; a docker's son becoming a doctor, for example

2 Intragenerational mobility – where someone changes their social position in their own lifetime, as, for example, when a clerk ends up as a manager

3 Stratum mobility – where an entire stratum or occupational group changes social position.

The topic of social mobility has been one of intense interest to sociologists as part of the wider debate as to how 'open' societies like ours really are. Is there equality of opportunity in Britain? Is privilege declining? And if so, with what effect? The first major mobility study in this country was by Professor David Glass and associates in 1949. It showed a good deal of intergenerational mobility but most of it was short-range and in the middle. There was a very high degree of elite self-recruitment in social classes I and II and a similar lack of movement at the bottom. The most recent major study was made during the 1970s by the Oxford Mobility Studies Group under John Goldthorpe. The group found a considerable increase in the amount of upward social mobility and a significant decline in the extent to which top positions are filled by the sons of existing elites. Such an expansion of opportunity, however, was not so much due to a more open social system as to changes in the occupational structure, with the expansion of white-collar jobs and a decline in manual ones.

Due to the low fertility rate of the existing middle classes, it was necessary to recruit the abler members of the working class. Hence the expansion of higher education and the move to comprehensive education in the 1960s. The overall picture of the British social structure today therefore is one of a diamond rather than triangular shape with an expanding and heterogeneous middle class and a shrinking, homogeneous working class. Yet the opportunity for movement is still very unequàl and the child from a social class V background has as little chance of going to university or getting a top job as he would have had in the 1930s.

Sociologists differ in their interpretations of the social effects of increased social mobility. Whilst functionalists and liberal writers applaud it as a means to a more meritocratic and classless society (or at least as a safety valve releasing underlying social tensions) Marxist writers see it as an illusion and a threat. It hides the 'real' gap between the classes, that between owners and non-owners of the means of production rather than that between manual and non-manual workers. The limited mobility that does occur is merely a means of 'creaming-off' the ablest of the working class to help run the capitalist system, so leaving the rest of the proletariat leaderless and divided. It helps legitimise capitalism by making the system seem fair (promotion according to ability) and classless whilst in reality the class system is simply reproduced. The 'myth' of social mobility in advanced capitalist societies, argue Marxists, is thus another form of ideological control.

Comparisons of rates of mobility in other advanced countries are extremely difficult, as such societies are at very different stages of development. S.M. Miller's study in 1960 found mobility in Britain, Sweden, America and the USSR to be similar. More recent studies see Austria and Sweden as the most 'open' western societies, West Germany and Japan the least and Britain and America in between. Others argue that socialist societies are more open than capitalist.

The main conclusions arising from all studies of social mobility though are that they face major problems of analysis and that their conclusions are highly tenuous:

(a) The problems of deciding and evaluating social scales. Few sociologists are satisfied with the Registrar General's scale and various refinements have ▶

been made (e.g. the Hall-Jones and Goldthorpe-Hope scales) in an attempt to add power, status and wealth to occupation. None, however, fulfils the Marxist demand for a scale that juxtaposes the bourgeoisie and the proletariat, nor the feminist for female occupations. And where do the un-employed fit in?

(b) The problems caused by the shifting nature of both social and occupational scales over time. For example, in Victorian times the vicar was an important person and the advertising executive did not exist.

(c) The problems of determining the point at which intra- and inter-generational mobility is measured. At what point in the son's or father's career do you compare them?

What such research does show is that despite the appearance of 'mass movement' even in such classless societies as Russia and America mobility is relatively limited, short-range and dependent more on change in the occupational structure than on the elevation of individuals and groups. The majority accept the class they are born into and it is their attitudes rather than those of competition and ambition that characterise most social systems.

See also CLASS, CASTE, FEUDALISM, EMBOURGEOISEMENT.

'used to eat and drink like a dog ... she would gnaw a big bone on the ground and rub it at times in order to separate the meat from the bone.'

Cases like this vividly illustrate the effects of a lack of human contact and learning at a critical time in human life. All people have an inborn capacity to develop into fully mature members of society but whether they actually do so depends on their upbringing and whether they are taught to form social relationships with others.

Socialisation, though, is not just part of childhood. It is a lifelong experience in which various social agencies have a part to play:

1 Obviously, the family is of crucial importance because infanthood and childhood are such formative stages of life and because the relationships of

is for

SOCIALISATION

Human behaviour — unlike that of other species — is based more on learning than on instinct. We have to learn to be human; it doesn't just come naturally.

In particular, we have to learn speech and self-control. As we grow up we are taught the culture, language, norms and ways of behaving of the particular society into which we are born. So powerful is this socialisation process, that by adulthood we will have internalised these rules and expectations to the degree that they become a part of our personality and character.

Consider how different a person you would be had you been born in China, into the Royal Family or even born a member of the opposite sex. Or if you had been brought up like the 'wolf children' — Amala and Kamala, girls aged two and eight — who were discovered in a wolf den in Bengal in 1920. Kamala, for example

parent and child are so intimate and emotional. A great deal of learning here is not through direct instruction but example, imitation and interaction — in particular, learning male and female roles from 'Mummy' and 'Daddy'. As the child grows up, though, it mixes with other children both in its own family and outside. The influence of such 'peer groups' can both reinforce parental teaching and provide alternative standards of behaviour.

2 At school, formal socialisation takes place, teaching the skills, knowledge and habits considered vital for survival and progress in society — reading, writing and numeracy, for example. But the child also learns a 'hidden' curriculum — ways of 'handling' those in authority, so as to gain their approval.

3 Adult socialisation is a similar combination of formal and informal ▶

learning, of working out the best way to survive in society. As members of various social groups (the office, the golf club, the union, the local pub), people go through a whole series of socialising processes, some reinforcing the dominant norms of society, some working against them.

4   On a broader level we are all subject to the powerful ideological teachings of the church and/or the mass media.

Sociologists like Charles Cooley have therefore distinguished between PRIMARY and SECONDARY socialisation, between the learning that takes place in such small and intimate groups as the family and peer group and that which is more direct, formal and impersonal, as occurs in schools. Sociologists like the Newsoms in Britain (*Patterns of Care in our Urban Society*, 1963) and Bronfenbrenners in America have highlighted the crucial differences in the way middle and working-class parents bring up their children and the way such upbringing influences such children's attitudes to school, authority and the future.

Different sociological perspectives have put a different emphasis on the power and effect of socialisation:

Functionalists like Talcott Parsons see socialisation as a key means to getting the individual to fit into society by learning and internalising its norms and values and preparing for future roles.

Inadequate socialisation produces non-conformity, inefficiency and so disrupts the social system.

Marxists too see socialisation as a moulding process imposed from above but based not on any inherent social consensus but on the attitudes and values necessary for the efficiency, profitability and stability of capitalism. The media, schools and even the family are part of the ideological apparatus used by the bourgeoisie to condition people to consume material goods and accept capitalism as inevitable and natural, and alternatives as radical and threatening.

Interactionists in contrast emphasise the active involvement of the individual, even as a child, in the socialisation process. Different individuals experience substantially different upbringing, react differently even to the same influences and interpret social roles differently. In the interactionist view, society does not control the individual like a puppet or mould him or her like plastic. Rather the individual is capable of conscious involvement and choice.

Such a discussion is part of the broader debate over whether human behaviour is predominately innate and instinctive or heavily influenced by upbringing and environment. Thus socialisation is a crucial sociological concept and a key part of any discussion on culture or social control.

See also CULTURE, FUNCTIONALISM, INTERACTIONISM, NORMS, SOCIAL CONTROL, SUB-CULTURE.

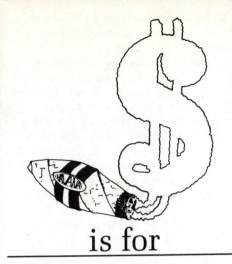

is for
STATUS

Status can be most simply defined as a person's social position as defined by others and/or accorded certain prestige or esteem. Status may be formal – the prestige gained from holding a particular social position, job or role – or informal – the esteem accorded by others to a particular individual for their special talents or skills. For example, whoever is Prime Minister or Headmaster automatically has high social prestige but Jimmy Jones has to gain the respect of his classmates by his ability to tell jokes or fight. Status is similarly linked to social ROLES (see p. 92) and so involves certain expectations. Upon marrying, a woman gains a certain social esteem but also certain responsibilities towards her husband – as a doctor does to his patients or a teacher to his pupils. Different occupations enjoy different social status. Compare, for example, the status of a doctor and a dustman. But even within a particular occupation there is a 'status hierarchy'; for example, amongst doctors a consultant has higher prestige than a general practitioner and amongst members of the cleansing department, dustcart drivers are something of an elite.

Status can therefore be defined as ASCRIBED and/or ACHIEVED. Ascribed statuses are those social positions or roles which an individual is born into and have little control over. For example, being born a member of the Royal Family in Britain automatically places you at the peak of our social structure. Being born black or a woman is likely in most societies to put you in an inferior position. Achieved status is that gained by the individual's own efforts during their lifetime, their ability to rise up the social or occupational scale. Some individuals or groups try to improve their status position by adopting the lifestyles, 'status symbols' or behaviour of groups above them. For example, the working-class family that buys its own home and votes Conservative as a means of entry to the middle class. Or the occupational group that seeks the status of becoming a profession by changing its title (e.g. bookies calling themselves Turf Accountants).

Social status is thus culturally defined. It depends on what a particular society or social group considers important – or on the power of a particular group or individual to control the allocation of prestige. Status can change over time. Consider for example the high prestige of the old in many ancient civilisations with their position today in societies like ours. Moreover status is obviously closely linked to other forms of social stratification such as power, wealth and class and we can talk not only of a STATUS HIERARCHY but of STATUS GROUPS, groups which, like classes, comprise people of similar social position and lifestyle. With such positions go STATUS SYMBOLS such as the Rolls-Royce of the wealthy and the Harley Davidson of the Hell's Angels leader. However, status is a very delicate and tenuous form of social stratification, not only because it overlaps and cuts across broader social classifications such as class and education but because it depends on SUBJECTIVE as well as OBJECTIVE factors. This may lead to reverse ranking. For ▶

STATUS (continued)

example, whilst non-manual groups generally enjoy a higher social position than manual ones, many 'workers' look down on 'pen pushers' like civil servants – a form of 'inverted snobbery'. Similarly most people hold not one but a variety of social statuses, some of which reinforce each other, some of which conflict – as for example in being a Cabinet Minister from a working-class background and so finding it difficult to truly fit in with upper-class, public school 'types'.

The sociological analysis of status – and many of the above concepts – derive mainly from the work of the German sociologist Max Weber. He sought to show that analyses of people's behaviour and social position solely in terms of CLASS – like that by Karl Marx – take too narrow a perspective. Whilst agreeing that a person's economic position was a key factor in their class position, he sought to show that status and class were not inevitably the same. Today, for example, clergymen are low down the pay-scale but still enjoy distinctive social respect. Similarly 'winning the pools' does not inevitably lead to high social status. Just as classes

often conflict and use exclusion tactics to preserve their privileged position so too, he argued, do 'status groups'.

He saw Marx's analysis of social structure into two classes as too simple and crude, arguing that factors like status cut across class lines and fragmented classes internally. Studies like those by David Lockwood, John Rex and Ken Roberts have shown, for example, the way that the working class can be divided into different types (respectable and rough, proletarian and deferential); that being black often cuts you off from your own class and the way the middle class is fragmented into a variety of 'middle classes'.

Thus in Weber's view, status was as important a source of social stratification and conflict and as crucial an influence on behaviour and lifestyle as class. In societies like ours where there is a fair amount of social mobility, the fit between class and status is fairly loose while in more rigid societies like those with a caste system there is greater CONGRUENCY. Similarly those who move up the social scale often find it difficult to 'fit in'; for example, the miner's son who goes to Oxford University. This is called STATUS DISSONANCE.

STATUS is thus a key concept in sociological analysis of social structure, behaviour and self-esteem.

See also CASTE, CLASS, POWER.

others can be very dangerous because:

1 We believe them to be true and so gain a false and distorted view of other people
2 They are used to promote and justify prejudice, discrimination and even persecution of minorities — as happened with the Jews in Nazi Germany.

Stereotypes are learnt and reinforced in the same way as other forms of social knowledge — through socialisation and social institutions like the media; For example, the idea that men are strong, decisive, rational and confident and women weak, passive, emotional and warm is part of the stereotype that men should be breadwinners and that a woman's place is in the home with her children. Evidence to the contrary — scientific evidence of girls' intelligence, or the ability of Mrs Thatcher as Prime Minister — tends to be ignored.

The problem is that stereotypes have a strong tendency to be proved true — a sort of inbuilt self-fulfilment. For example,

is for

STEREOTYPES

A stereotype is a widespread, exaggerated, often emotional view or belief, loosely based on fact about a particular group or society that becomes fixed in the public mind, is repeated without change and is resistant to factual evidence to the contrary. For example, the popular belief that the Irish are stupid and that the Scots are mean may be true of a few people but cannot be true of a whole nation.

These images are part of our social language, part of the means by which we try to make sense of a complicated and varied world. Some are quite mild and harmless — that the French have a diet of frog's legs, for example, and the Italians live on spaghetti and ice cream — but

research has shown that some members of the police have a stereotype of criminals as young, male, working-class, probably black and living in the inner city. So they concentrate their attentions on such groups, inevitably find the crime they are looking for, and are proved right. Moreover the stereotype criminal — those in prison — tends to dominate our image (and sociological theories) of crime, so diverting attention from the less visible yet equally serious crimes of, say, white-collar workers or top businessmen and politicians. Similarly once such a stereotype has developed, youngsters in inner cities start living up to it, so reinforcing the cycle of misunderstanding. Girls and boys similarly try ▶

STEREOTYPES (continued)

living up to images of the ideal housewife or 'strong' man.

Sociologists point out that stereotypes usually rest on an underlying structure of power by which one group in society seeks to keep another in its place by promoting a distorted image of it. For example, the stereotype that blacks are inferior, unintelligent, uncivilised and childlike was not only used to justify the slavery of colonial days but also underlies the racial discrimination of today. Similarly, it is argued, our stereotypes of women are based on a structure of power by which men seek to keep women 'in their place'.

It is 'patriarchy' not biology that underlies the different social roles of men and women, argue feminists (see GENDER, p. 42). Similarly fear and a lack of understanding underlie popular views of many other 'deviant' groups — homosexuals, punks, even strikers, and are used by those in power to misinform, divide and scare ordinary people. Consider for example media campaigns against 'social security scroungers', communists and Arthur Scargill.

Thus stereotypes are not only part of our language but part of our IDEOLOGY (see p. 50) and our structure of power.

See also LABELLING, DEVIANCE.

is for
SUB-CULTURE

society's culture is an amalgam of the various cultural elements within it.

When a group of people within a society have a lifestyle that includes aspects of the main culture, but also some cultural elements not found in other groups, this is known as a sub-culture. The most obvious sub-cultures in Britain today are those of the various ethnic groups who have settled here, and the young.

Counter-cultures are lifestyles, sets of beliefs and values that develop in opposition to the main culture, challenging its beliefs, ideals and institutions. Counter-cultures often develop amongst groups who feel isolated, threatened or who have a common interest to defend against outsiders. The sub-cultures of the young, of ethnic and deviant groups seem to many to be of this type. The youth-cultures of the

Few if any large-scale societies have a single culture that is shared and accepted by everyone. Very often what is called a

1950s, 1960s and onwards represented a rejection of authority and of conventional standards – of dress, music and morality. But even here there is a distinct class-difference. The working-class rebellion was symbolised by such cults as teddy boys, Hell's Angels, skinheads and more recently punks. As Jeff Clarke argues, their styles of dress were, in many ways exaggerated versions of traditional working-class clothing, and their aggressiveness was a reaction to their rejection by middle-class society, especially the police, teachers and town-planners. Unable to hit back directly they either sought to shock or looked for scapegoats like immigrants. Middle-class adolescents also expressed their rebellion through clothes and music but generally they were less aggressive and more questioning – especially of the values of capitalist society. The student rebellions of the 1960s, Woodstock, flower power and the commune movement questioned such issues as Vietnam, nuclear war and civil rights.

However, many sociologists question whether such 'appearances' really represented a single sub-culture, especially as the vast majority of youngsters soon pass through this phase of adolescent rebellions, marry and settle down to jobs and careers. In their view the media and big business exaggerated such cultural differences as a means to creating a whole new market for clothes, records, etc.

This argument is part of the functionalist/Marxist debate on youth culture. Functionalist writers like S. Einsestadt (*From Generation to Generation*, 1956) see the period of extended adolescence in modern societies, created by increased education and leisure, as leaving young people today in an ambiguous and insecure position. They are neither children nor adults; they are about to leave the family and home and yet have no job or position in adult society to go to. The emergence of a separate 'youth' culture provides temporary stability and an alternative value-system during this period of transition. Young people turn to each other for security and so there also develops an apparent 'generation gap'.

Marxists reject such a picture of modern youth not only because functionalism presents a consensual and harmonious picture of society but because it depicts age as the only real division in society and a temporary one at that. The 'worlds' of both adults and the young are portrayed as integrated and homogeneous wholes. Internal divisions, particularly of class, are totally ignored. Yet, argue Marxists, class divides the world of youth just as effectively as it divides that of adults. Despite the appearance of classlessness, middle-class youth and working-class youth are, in reality, little different in terms of attitudes, values and aspirations from their parents, but very different from each other. Writers like Mungham and Pearson (*Working Class Youth Cultures*, 1976) believe these two 'classes' of youth inhabit separate sub-cultures. They see the skinhead cult of the 1970s both as a working-class reaction to the flower power of middle-class students in the 1960s and as a reaffirmation – albeit an exaggerated one based on bovver boots and braces – of such youngsters' working-class roots – a strategy of resistance by the young 'proletariat' against a system of authority in which they are part of the subordinate class. Possibly ethnic groups represent an even more substantial example of sub-culture. Such groups have preserved their own ways of life, languages and traditions as both a source of security and identity in a 'foreign' land. In societies like Britain and America white ethnic groups have generally assimilated fairly easily into mainstream society even if there were problems of language (e.g. Irish in Britain, Italians, Greeks and Germans in America) Many black groups, because they are more visibly different, have not found it so easy; faced by prejudice, discrimination and rejection they tend to withdraw almost into a 'siege mentality'. Rather than accept the idea that they are in any way inferior they have developed ▶

SUB-CULTURE (continued)

various Black Power movements in both these countries (e.g. the Rastafarians, Black Panthers).

Various deviant groups — homosexuals, drug addicts, criminals, prostitutes — are further obvious examples to which the concept sub-culture would seem highly applicable. But it can also illuminate the 'ways of life, attitudes and values' of a wide variety of less obvious groups — the working class and the middle class, the old and even the poor. The anthropologist Oscar Lewis proposed the idea of a culture of poverty — a sense of marginality, helplessness, inferiority, fatalism and social fragmentation — that is one reason why the poor find it so difficult to break out of poverty. Feminists have talked of a culture of femininity that imprisons women in their traditional roles, in marriage and in the home and so keeps them subordinate to men. Educational researchers like David Hargreaves have identified the 'delinquent' sub-culture that develops in the bottom streams of schools as a reaction to being labelled failures.

The uses of this concept are therefore endless but all too easily it can be misused. Superficial differences in dress or behaviour are taken as evidence of a distinct way of life where no such depth exists. Moreover a true sub-culture is meant to be related to the dominant culture of society, but often it is difficult to determine not only which part of a sub-culture is distinct, and which mainstream, but also what are the main characteristics of the 'dominant cultures' in societies so diverse as America and even Britain.

See also CULTURE, GROUPS, NORMS, PEER GROUP, SOCIALISATION.

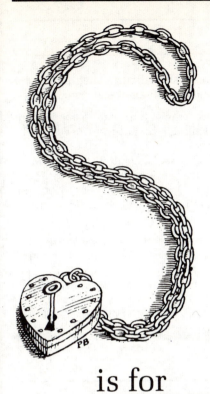

is for
SUBJECTIVITY

Subjectivity refers to people's feelings, emotions and ideas, to their personal point of view and their motives – be they those of the subjects of a particular study or those of the researcher himself. Though traditional sociology in its search for OBJECTIVITY (see p. 69) has sought to eliminate all irrational and unmeasurable factors, there have been strains within the discipline which maintain that a true and full understanding of social behaviour is impossible without at least some consideration of personal and subjective feelings. Many writers have argued that at heart people are emotional rather than rational creatures and that civilisation merely represents a thin veneer of restraint and order over their innermost passions. Rational explanations are thus often little more than glib justifications for behaviour that is in essence based on the heart rather than the head.

The strongest assault on traditional scientific sociology has come from phenomenologists. They believe that since society and social behaviour are basically subjective, so our understanding of them must be similarly based if any kind of valid interpretation is to be achieved. Objectivity and 'value-freedom' are impossible because, by definition, researchers, too, are products of their own cultural and ideological backgrounds. Rather than imposing their own 'rational and impartial' opinions on a given social situation or event, they should, as far as is possible, allow the participants to speak for themselves. How else will we ever understand such apparently 'mindless' behaviour as vandalism and suicide? Even our legal system puts especial emphasis on a person's motives. Hence the emphasis in phenomenological research on such techniques as 'participant observation'.

But 'mainstream' sociologists, too, have always recognised the value of subjectivity. The 'founding father', Max Weber, for instance, placed emphasis on *verstehen* (the ability of a researcher to put himself in his subject's place).

There have also been modern studies in which the notion of subjectivity plays an integral part. F.M. Martin made a famous analysis in the early 1950s ('Some Subjective Aspects of Social Stratification', in D.V. Glass and J.R. Hall, *Social Mobility in Britain* 1954) of subjective class-consciousness and the extent to which people's own view of their position in the social class hierarchy differs from that to which a sociologist would have assigned them. Many of his sample saw themselves as being in a higher social class than that assigned to them by the Hall-Jones scale. Goldthorpe and Lockwood's widely-quoted ▶

SUBJECTIVITY (continued)

critique of the embourgeoisement thesis (see p. 30) showed that though affluent workers may have appeared to be becoming middle-class in terms of such objective factors as their income, they did not actually 'feel' nor wish to be bourgeois.

Thus phenomenologists have sought to reverse the traditional sociological perspective by letting the subjects of a study speak for themselves rather than getting an 'objective' researcher to do it for them. Such an approach has helped re-balance much sociological work and force researchers to face up to the influence of their own values and attitudes on their work. Inevitably, though, such an emphasis on subjectivity has been criticised as:

1 being unscientific and making it impossible for sociology to develop as a science.
2 reducing sociology to little more than a series of self-accounts by a variety of social groups, with no overriding theoretical framework or independent analysis.

The recent work of sociologists like Anthony Giddens is one attempt to follow Weber's lead in trying to combine objectivity and subjectivity in the study of class.

See also: OBJECTIVITY, IDEOLOGY, POSITIVISM, PHENOMENOLOGY.

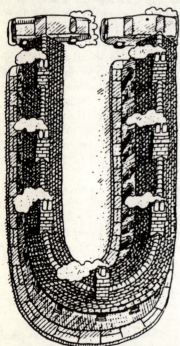 is for

URBAN-ISATION

towns and cities of a certain size has grown.

The growth of densely populated cities and their suburbs is a relatively recent phenomenon. Though the world's first cities were probably developed over 5000 years ago, the growth of fully urbanised societies began 100 to 150 years ago. In the United States, for example, only 5% of the population was classified as urban in 1790 whereas by 1900 the figure had risen to 40% and by 1970 to 74%. It is estimated that by the year 2000 well over half the world's population will be residents of cities with populations of 100 000 or more.

The word 'urban' refers to those of or in a town and urbanisation is the process by which the proportion of people living in

In the most advanced nations, urbanisation has reached the point of METRO-

POLITISATION whereby the largest cities start swallowing up nearby satellite towns and become major regional and industrial centres. In Britain today for example over 40% of the population live in one of the seven major CONURBATIONS like Merseyside or Greater London.

Very briefly, the main causes of the massive migration in nineteenth-century Britain from the countryside to the city can be listed as:

the Agricultural Revolution and the enclosure movement which drove the peasantry and small farmer off the land; the Industrial Revolution and its factories, mines and mills which attracted such workers into the towns in search of better wages and bright lights; the population explosion of the nineteenth century dramatically increased the workforce and towns were now the main source of work as this was where industry was based.

The twentieth century, however, has seen a dramatic move *out* of the towns and cities, a flight from the inner city to the suburbs, due to such developments as:

- the Transport Revolution − the growth of public (buses, rail) and private (the car) transport, enabling people to commute between home and work;
- the Housing Revolution − the growth of mass housing, public and private, mainly in the suburbs and on the outskirts of cities;
- slum clearance and redevelopment programmes demolished inner-city slums and moved the inhabitants to New Towns and council estates outside the major cities;
- the relocation of industry − twentieth-century industries have generally not had to base themselves in cities due to new production methods and transport systems like the rail and motorway networks so new factories tend to be in the greener areas outside town and cities.

There has also been a significant shift of industry and so of people from the North to the South.

The shape of the city has changed, too. In the early industrial cities factories and businesses were situated in the centre surrounded by the terraces of the skilled working class. Beyond them lay the suburban houses of the middle classes and circling them the great mansions and estates of the gentry and the prosperous businessmen and merchants. The nineteenth- and twentieth-century shift out of the inner city left behind the slums of the twilight zones and ghettoes which attracted the poor, the single and the destitute and immigrant groups, areas that even today are seen as 'breeding grounds' of crime, vandalism and drug addiction. There is some evidence, mainly in America, of a trend amongst the younger middle-class groups to moving back into the major cities, a process called GENTRIFICATION. But there is an even stronger trend especially in Britain to move even further out, to COMMUTER VILLAGES and retirement centres on the coast.

Sociologists have tended to see the great urban centres as examples of both the best and the worst features of industrialisation and modern life.

The early theories of the city were mainly those of the Community Studies tradition, the ideas that sprang from the writings of Ferdinand Tonnies, Emile Durkheim and Louis Wirth, of contrasting rural and urban 'Ways of life', of urban environments leading to a 'loss of community' and a breakdown of social order (see COMMUNITY, p. 17, for details).

Urban Sociology as a distinct discipline, however, stems more from the work of R.E. Park and the Chicago School of Sociologists and geographers in the 1920s. Using the idea of HUMAN ECOLOGY they analysed the city as a sort of social organism with a life of its own and they explained the pattern of housing evident in early industrial cities as a sort of Darwinian struggle for survival in which the least 'fit', the poor, were left behind in ▶

the inner city. Such zones of transition, especially in America, fostered a whole variety of ethnic cultures and ways of life, some of which involved criminal lifestyles and social disorganisation (Little Sicily, Chinatown). Modern urban sociology generally rejects such functionalist and ecological theories in favour of those putting greater emphasis on power and conflict, the power of certain groups to shape our cities. Such radical sociology is mainly based on the theories of either Max Weber or Karl Marx. A Weberian analysis sees the city as a sort of marketplace for conflict between competing classes.

1 In 1967 John Rex and Robert Moore put forward the idea of housing classes as a way of explaining the distribution of housing and class and why ethnic groups tended to be left behind in the inner city (*Race, Community and Conflict*, 1976). Low income, lack of residency qualifications and white prejudice force such groups to withdraw into ghetto areas almost as a form of protection. The attitudes and treatment of such groups by housing officials and building society managers increase segregation.

2 R.E. Pahl advanced the idea of urban managerialism, that the key figures in urban life are those officials who control the distribution of housing, education, welfare and so on (building society and council house managers, town planners, education officers, etc.), plus such figures as property developers, bankers and shopkeepers. Under criticism that such figures were only 'middle' managers under the control of Big Government and Big Business, he refined his theory into one of the Corporate State.

3 Marxist analyses go even further. For them the 'top dogs' who shape our cities are the bourgeoisie, and the city is simply another arena for the 'class struggle'. The worst features of our cities are the worst features of capitalism. The Spanish sociologist Manuel Castells (*The Urban Question*, 1977), for example, saw the urban protest movements of the 1960s and 1970s over race, civil rights, housing and the environment as a new form of class struggle, one over goods of collective consumption (rather than over pay and conditions as in the workplace). Such goods include public housing, transport, education and welfare provided by the bourgeoisie via the modern state to keep the workers happy and healthy. However, during periods of economic crisis like the 1970s and 1980s, the capitalist state has to cut back and this hits not only the poor and working class but the middle classes. Thus such urban protests were a mixture of classes and Castells hoped that they could be integrated into the traditional class struggle, create urban crises and so help cause the collapse of capitalism. However, amid mass unemployment such protests have declined and there never was evidence of the middle classes joining a proletarian revolution.

4 More recent analyses both by Weberians and Marxists tend to concentrate on URBAN POLITICS, for example, the present government's increased control of local government finance (RATE-CAPPING) – the struggle between central and local government as in Liverpool.

Urban sociology has also taken a particular interest in the INNER CITY especially after the riots of 1981. Initially writers in this field saw the inner city as a problem area (crime, poor housing, poverty, unemployment) which bred its own problems and so needed solutions that could break the cycle of poverty of the people living there. So governments in both Britain and America (especially after the race riots of the 1960s) poured resources and manpower into such areas (EPAs, Headstart Programme, War on Poverty), with limited effect. Modern analyses generally reject such 'area-based' approaches because:

(a) There is more poverty outside the inner city than is in it so such a concentration of resources is missing most of its target

(b) The real causes of inner-city deprivation are not the area itself or the people living there but the economic policies of successive governments and of the big corporations. National and local government programmes of slum clearance, New Towns, etc. have taken the heart out of the city, moved the people, the shops and the jobs whilst the relocation of industry to the outskirts (or to the Third World countries) creates mass unemployment and degeneration. The withdrawal of multinationals like Dunlop, British American Tobacco and Massey Ferguson has turned cities like Liverpool into social and industrial wastelands. Marxist writers see this as just one more example of capitalist exploitation and irresponsibility.

The Labour Government's 1977 White Paper recognised that the only real solution was a coordinated programme of inner-city regeneration via housing and education as well as economic policy but the present Conservative Government, as part of its overall strategy, puts its faith in private enterprise (Enterprise Zones) and cuts in local government spending. The city in advanced industrial societies is thus today as crucial a social problem as it was in the nineteenth century.

See also COMMUNITY.

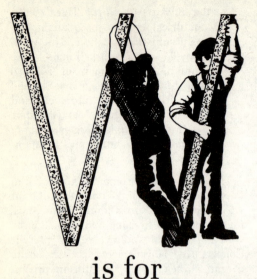

is for

WORKING CLASS

collar jobs, about 50% of adult males are now defined as working-class. As the *Oxford Mobility Study* (1972) showed that the British working class is shrinking and increasingly homogeneous as few 'outsiders' are recruited or allowed into it and as the sons of such workers move up into non-manual occupations. As always, a key problem with such objective classifications is subjective class-consciousness. As F.M. Martin ('Some Subjective Aspects of Stratification' in D.V. Glass and J.R. Hall *Social Mobility in Britain*, 1954) found even back in the 1950s, as many as one in three manual workers did not consider themselves 'working-class' and recent studies show a similar volatility of class-consciousness.

This is a term usually used to refer to those who do MANUAL WORK, who work with their hands in such 'productive' industries as coal, steel, and agriculture. Whilst such a definition puts the working class beneath the middle class, it also embodies a sense of worth, purpose and pride enabling such 'real' workers as miners to feel superior not only to the 'lower classes' and those in less traditional industries but to white-collar workers such as clerks who simply 'shuffle paper'.

As outlined in the definition of CLASS, descriptions of the working class vary according to the theoretical perspective involved. The primarily descriptive classification of the Registrar General categorises the working class(es) as manual occupations, skilled, semi-skilled and unskilled — social classes IIIM, IV, and V.

Whilst in the early twentieth century the overwhelming mass of the population could be classified as working-class (75% of employed population in 1977), with the decline of traditional manual occupations and the growth of automation and white-

Recent sociological debates on the working class in advanced capitalist societies have centred on its changing nature and role. Is the modern working class disintegrating or growing? Is it becoming more united and class-conscious or less so? Are such working-class organisations as the trades unions or the Labour Party means to radical change or have they become institutionalised and part of modern capitalism? Theories of a new working class, of a variety of working classes, started with the EMBOURGEOISEMENT THESIS of the early 1960s, the idea of affluent skilled workers becoming MIDDLE-CLASS (see p. 66). Though Goldthorpe and Lockwood's study of car and chemical workers (*The Affluent Worker*, 1968) is generally seen as a rejection of this theory, they did acknowledge that such workers were distinct from the traditional working class and constituted a new PRIVATISED working class. In the view of Weberian writers like Ralf Dahrendorf the modern working class is highly fragmented, heterogeneous and in many ways 'decomposing' via changes in technology, the decline of traditional industries and the way trade unions today are more a means to maintaining differentials of pay and status between workers rather than uniting them against capitalist employers. Certain craft and skilled groups of workers in key positions in the economy and powerful unions such as the miners and printers consider themselves among the ARISTO-CRACY OF LABOUR. Analyses of subjective class attitudes such as that by David Lockwood ('Sources of Variation in Working-Class Images of Society' in M. Bulmer's *Working-Class Images of Society*, 1975) further showed a variety, not a unity, of working class-consciousnesses (deferential, proletarian and privatised).

Marxist writers tend to look more for evidence that the British working class is turning from being a 'class in itself' to being one 'for itself', that it is growing in size, unity, class-consciousness and militancy to the point of being able to overthrow the bourgeoisie (see MARXISM, p. 61). Their definition is broader than that of the Registrar General and Weberian writers and is encompassed in the term PROLETARIAT, the non-owners of the means of production; though they too distinguish between REAL workers and the lumpenproletariat (tramps, vagrants, prostitutes). Many Marxist writers would include in the ranks of the proletariat the lower middle class (supervisory and white collar staff). Amid the financial crises, the mass unemployment, the growth of union militancy and the apparently inevitable movement towards automation and deskilling, writers like Harry Braverman (*Labor and Monopoly Capitalism* 1974) have advanced the 'proletarianisation thesis' (see p. 85), the view that the distinctions between workers and white-collar employees are secondary to their common experience of exploitation and powerlessness.

Moreover, as Westergaard and Resler (*Class in a Capitalist Society*, 1976) argue, working-class differentials are insignificant in comparison with the gulf in incomes, lifechances, freedoms and security between manual and non-manual workers. Trade unionism helps workers to get a better share of the capitalist 'cake' but only in a socialist society would the means of production be communally-owned, with workers enjoying real equality and the true fruits of their labour. The problem is how to raise the consciousness of the working class as a whole above such internal divisions, conservatism and ideological submission to capitalist values and attitudes. Though the miners' strike of 1974 and the apparent power of the unions in the 1970s seemed to herald the collapse of capitalism, the mass unemployment of the 1980s, the present weaknesses of the unions and Labour Party, and especially the 1979 and 1983 elections in which a Tory government was returned with the help of working-class votes, have forced such writers to considerably reanalyse their theories of the modern working class. Moreover, where do blacks and females fit into modern analyses of the working class? As an integral part of the proletariat, a further source of internal division or as an 'underclass'?

See also CLASS, MARXISM, PROLETARIAT.

EXAMINATION QUESTIONS

Every major examining board in Sociology sets questions requiring precise definitions and/or brief explanations of key sociological terms, concepts and theories. The definitions and summaries contained in this book cover a wide range of sociology syllabuses. It offers an invaluable study and revision aid for those preparing for public examinations in this and related areas of Social Studies/ Sciences – as well as providing a useful guide to those undertaking introductory or basic courses.

GCSE

EAST ANGLIAN EXAMINATIONS BOARD
LONDON REGIONAL EXAMINING BOARD
JOINT O LEVEL/CSE EXAMINATION

Part I, Section C

6 **(a)** What is the difference between criminal and non-criminal deviance? (3 marks)

   (b) Give TWO examples of non-criminal deviance and explain why each is considered deviant. (5 marks)

   (c) 'Laws vary from time to time and from place to place.' Why do laws change? (7 marks)

Part II

7 How far is it true to say that a distinct youth culture exists in Britain? (15 marks)

8 To what extent have sociologists shown that there are differences between living in urban and rural communities? (15 marks)

9 How important are pressure groups in political decision-making? (15 marks)

10 'Industrialisation has affected the family.' Discuss. (15 marks)

11 To what extent is organised religion still important in Britain today? (15 marks)

12 'Women are still second-class citizens'. Discuss. (15 marks)

Section C

5 **(a)** Describe TWO different ways in which 'social class' may be defined. (4 marks)

(b) How does 'social class' differ from ONE other form of social stratification? $\quad$ (5 *marks*)

(c) Explain how social class influences any TWO of the following areas: $\quad$ (6 *marks*)
- (i) voting behaviour
- (ii) work
- (iii) education
- (iv) leisure

(Specimen paper, Spring 1984)

WELSH JOINT EDUCATION COMMITTEE $\qquad$ **CYD-BWYLLGOR ADDYSG CYMRU**

JOINT O LEVEL/CSE EXAMINATION

1 Write in the words which are missing in the following sentences: $\quad$ (6×½)

(a) Ridicule is a form of .... social control.

(b) The process whereby a person changes his social class is known as social ....

(c) A fairly permanent group with intimate face-to-face relationships is known as a .... group.

(d) The position occupied by a person in society is known as ....

(e) The range of socially learned characteristics which are passed from one generation to the next is known as that society's ....

(f) A .... society is one whose system of social stratification does not allow persons to change what they are born into.

2 Study the following carefully. For each definition in Column A find the most appropriate term in Column B. Then record your answer by writing the number from Column B before its appropriate definition in Column A. $\quad$ (10×½)

COLUMN A	COLUMN B
(a) An established practice and usage which governs the relationships between individuals and groups.	1 ascription
(b) The system of social stratification which operates in Britain.	2 organisation
	3 elite
(c) A type of relationship characterised by indirect, contractual and impersonal contact.	4 authority
	5 sanctions
(d) A traditional practice in society.	6 socialisation
(e) The process of learning the ways of a society so as to be able to function within it.	7 function
	8 stereotype
(f) Any means used by a group to discourage deviant or non-conformist behaviour.	9 socialism
	10 secondary
(g) Power that is accepted as proper and legitimate by the majority of members of a group or society.	11 institution
	12 gender
(h) A status position one is born into.	13 belief
(i) That which refers to people's behaviour in groups.	14 perception
(j) Biased and oversimplified ideas about the characteristics of members of a particular social group.	15 class
	16 custom
	17 exchange
	18 interaction

3 Read the following passage and then answer the questions.

All societies have a system of social differentiation. In societies which are very close to subsistence level — that is, where people have to spend most of their time concentrating on survival — the socially different roles will tend to be few, and they will be very clear-cut. Age and sex are usually important as the basis of roles, and in a very simple social system they may be the only two factors. There are always certain jobs laid down as men's functions rather than women's, and there are always differences recognised between the young, and mature, and the old. These need not involve serious inequalities, but there is a widespread tendency in human societies for some individuals to be richer, more powerful, and of higher prestige than others. The role of child tends to be of low power and prestige, the role of wife tends to carry less power than a masculine role, and it is common in simple societies for leaders to have considerable power and prestige (even if they do not have greater wealth).

Every role carries with it a pattern of expectations as well as duties, responsibilities and privileges.

Lawton, D. *Investigating Society*

5

10

15

(a) In Sociology what is meant by the following terms which are used in the above passage?
   (i) social differentiation   (line 1)   (2)
   (ii) power   (line 11)   (2)

(b) What do you understand by 'age and sex are usually important as the basis   (2)
of roles'?   (line 4)

(c) Give an example of a role which is based on
   (i) age . . . .   (½)
   (ii) sex . . . .   (½)

(d) Give a brief description of the 'expectations' which relate to your role as a   (3)
pupil (or student).

4 **(a)** Describe what is meant by:
   (i) participant observation,   (2)
   (ii) non-participant observation.   (2)

6 Explain the meaning of the following:
(a) interviewer bias,   (2)
(b) pilot study.   (2)

7 Describe the difference between the following pairs of terms:
(a) population and sample,   (2)
(b) pre-coded and open-ended items.   (2)

6 **(a)** Describe what is meant by 'alienation' in the context of work.   (3)

(b) Describe briefly any *two* social consequences (not alienation) of   (2×3)
technological changes in modern British industry.

(c) Discuss how a person's work may influence his/her leisure   (11)
activities.

7 **(a)** Describe and distinguish between   (i) caste, and   (3)
                                           (ii) class.   (3)

(b) Describe what is meant by 'embourgeoisement'. (3)

(c) Discuss what is meant by saying that life-styles vary with social class. (11)

8 (a) What is meant by 'urbanisation'? (3)

(b) Outline the characteristic social features of a 'neighbourhood'. (5)

(c) Discuss the contributions made by sociologists to our under-standing of any *two* problems associated with urbanisation. (6+6)

9 (a) Describe, with suitable examples, what is meant by
(i) movements, (3)
(ii) pressure groups. (3)

(b) State briefly the characteristic features of a 'bureaucracy'. (5)

(c) Explain what is meant by saying that 'the State has a monopoly of legitimate force'. (9)

10 'Deviance varies within societies, between societies, and over time.'
(a) Describe what is meant by 'deviance'. (3)

(b) State, with appropriate examples, what is meant by the above quotation. (6)

(c) Discuss the similarities and differences between morality and crime. (11)

(From two specimen papers)

MIDLAND EXAMINING GROUP

JOINT O LEVEL/CSE EXAMINATION

1 A Give the meaning of the following terms used in studies of society and in each case indicate at which point in an investigation they would be used:
(i) questionnaire   1 + 1
(ii) pie chart   1 + 1
(iii) hypothesis   1 + 1   6

B Write a paragraph about the use of sampling in sociological research, mentioning at least **two** of the types of sampling used.   5

2 A (i) Breaking the law is an example of 'deviance'. Explain the meaning of the term deviance.   2

(ii) Prison is one form of 'social control'. What is social control and why is its use an important part of all groups and societies?   4

(Specimen paper)

Alternative O-Level

UNIVERSITY OF LONDON

Part 2

5 **(a)** What are pressure groups? *(4 marks)*

   (b) Outline briefly the political role of three pressure groups. *(6 marks)*

   (c) 'Pressure groups allow a wide section of the population to participate in political decision-making.' Examine the accuracy of this statement. *(10 marks)*

(Total 20 marks)

9 Examine the process of large-scale movement out of inner-city areas into the suburbs and new towns in Britain.

11 **(a)** What is meant by the term 'labelling'? *(6 marks)*

   (b) Discuss and illustrate how the idea of labelling has been useful to sociologists in the study of deviance. *(14 marks)*

(Total 20 marks)

14 **(a)** What factors have sociologists suggested may be associated with work satisfaction? *(10 marks)*

   (b) How has the concept 'alienation' been used by sociologists to aid their understanding of differences in the way people experience their work? *(10 marks)*

(Total 20 marks)

15 **(a)** Explain what is meant by the concept 'social stratification'. *(6 marks)*

   (b) Discuss two types of social stratification within any one society. *(14 marks)*

(Total 20 marks)

16 Examine the sociological evidence associated with the proposition that: *(20 marks)*
   either **(a)** manual workers are becoming middle-class
   or **(b)** non-manual workers are becoming working-class.

(June 1983)

A Level

AEB (ASSOCIATED EXAMINING BOARD)

The following questions are taken from a wide variety of recent examination papers. The Examining Board and year are indicated.

1 THE EXPERIMENT
'Despite the popularity and undoubted usefulness of the laboratory method in the natural sciences, it is almost never used in sociology. The reasons are both practical and moral....

Sociologists have, however, used experimental techniques in broader, if less controlled contexts than the laboratory. Many of these, such as testing the effects of media violence or sex on attitudes and behaviour have tended to be psychological rather than sociological in nature.... The sociologist's "laboratory" could be said to be society itself. He wants to study how people actually behave, not how they might behave in the laboratory.'

(source: M.O'Donnell, *A New Introduction to Sociology*, 1981)

(a) Explain the 'popularity and undoubted usefulness' of the laboratory method in the natural sciences. (8 *marks*)

(b) Why is the laboratory method 'almost never used in sociology'? (9 *marks*)

(c) The comparative method (i.e. the comparing of societies or of groups within a society) has been advocated by some sociologists as an alternative to the laboratory method. Why might the comparative method be considered an alternative to the laboratory method? (8 *marks*)

(June 1983)

2 'Sociologists cannot justifiably claim to be objective'. Discuss.

(Nov. 1981)

3 Compare and contrast sociological approaches to the study of the professions.

(Nov. 1983)

4 'Western industrial societies are undergoing a process of secularisation'. Explain and discuss.

(June 1983)

5 Describe the patterns of social mobility in any one society. What importance might different sociologists attach to such patterns?

(Nov. 1981)

6 Outline the major sociological usages of the term 'community' and examine the view that changes in Western society have led to a 'loss of community'.

(Nov. 1983)

7 There has been a long-standing debate among social scientists about the form of the national powerstructure in contemporary western industrial societies. Evaluate the main positions taken in this debate.

(June 1983)

JMB (Joint Matriculation Board)

1 Define POSITIVISM.

(June 1981)

2 Write an essay on the nature of deviant behaviour. In your essay you should use the following terms, and any others which you think are appropriate:
(i) boundary (or system) maintenance

(ii)   social control
(iii) differential socialisation
(iv)   anomie

(June 1981)

3   Define the following terms:
(a) capitalism
(b) professional association.

(June 1981)

4   It has been claimed that 'social stratification has changed in the past 100 years from a simple two-class system to a new system of many varied levels'.
Explain fully the implications of this claim. What evidence is there to support and/or refute the assertion?

(June 1983)

5   Summarise the Marxian analysis of the structure of, and conflict within, society. Is there any evidence to show that Marx's analysis has contemporary relevance? What problems are there in basing a conflict perspective solely upon Marx's work?

(June 1983)

6   Using a range of case studies, illustrate the concepts and ideas which interactionist sociologists have used to study organisation. Point out the DISTINCTIVENESS of an interactionist approach.

(June 1983)

OXFORD LOCAL EXAMINATIONS

1   What do you understand by the 'dependence ratio'? Assess the major changes in the dependence ratio since 1945 and their social consequences.

(June 1983)

2   Does the increasing popularity of fringe religious groups indicate that secularisation is a myth?

(June 1983)

3   The 1970s witnessed a major decline in the influence of social class upon political behaviour, especially voting. Discuss.

(June 1983)

4   Compare and contrast any two theoretical perspectives on deviance.

(June 1983)

UNIVERSITY OF CAMBRIDGE LOCAL EXAMINATIONS SYNDICATE

1   The bundle of drives which is a human baby develops as a person only through relationships with others'. What are the principal aspects of this process?

(June 1983)

2 How useful are the concepts of 'rural' and 'urban' for the analysis of social behaviour?

(June 1983)

3 'The history of all hitherto existing society is the history of class struggles'. (K. Marx and F. Engels) Does this statement provide an adequate basis for explaining social change?

(June 1983)

4 How do slavery, caste and estate differ as forms of social stratification?

(June 1983)

5 'There is no way any social scientist can avoid assuming choices of value and implying them in his work as a whole'. (C. Wright Mills) Discuss.

(June 1983)

UNIVERSITY OF LONDON

1 Compare and contrast any two systems of social stratification.

(June 1983)

2 'Any theory of race relations must be a special case of some theory of social stratification'. Explain and discuss.

(June 1983)

3 'Formal agencies of social control become necessary when ties of kinship and community are eroded'. Discuss.

(June 1983)